THE ANATOMY OF THE SOUL

HISTORICAL ESSAYS IN THE PHILOSOPHY OF MIND

ANTHONY KENNY

Published in the U.S.A. 1973 by
HARPER & ROW PUBLISHERS, INC.
BARNES & NOBLE IMPORT DIVISION

© Anthony Kenny 1973

All Rights Reserved. No part of this publication may be reproduced, stored in a retrieval system, or transmitted, in any form or by any means, electronic, mechanical, photocopying, recording or otherwise, without the prior permission of Basil Blackwell & Mott Limited.

ISBN 06-493638-4

Printed in Great Britain

CONTENTS

Introduction vii

Mental Health in Plato's Republic 1

The Practical Syllogism and Incontinence 28

Aristotle on Happiness 51

Intellect and Imagination in Aquinas 62

Descartes on the Will 81

Cartesian Privacy 113

Appendix:
The History of Intention in Ethics 129

INTRODUCTION

One of the fascinations of philosophy is the way in which it combines the attractions of the arts with those of the sciences. The philosopher, like the chemist or the meteorologist, goes in pursuit of truth; yet classics in philosophy are not antiquated by succeeding research in the way that the works of even the greatest scientists are outdated by later discoveries. No one would now read Ptolemy to learn about the planets, but one need not be an antiquarian to read Plato any more than to read Homer. Yet when we read Plato we are constantly raising the questions we would raise of a scientist and not of a poet: are his conclusions true, and are the arguments he offers for them valid?

The unique nature of philosophy makes the history of philosophy unlike the history of any other pursuit. A historian of mathematics does not *qua* historian do mathematics; a historian of painting need not be by profession a painter. But a historian of philosophy, unless he is to restrict himself to quotation and biography, cannot help doing philosophy. It is obvious enough that a man who knows no philosophy will be a bad historian of philosophy just as a man who is totally ignorant of medicine will be unable to write the history of medicine; but the connection between medicine and its history is a far looser one than that between philosophy and history of philosophy. For his very task as historian forces the historian of philosophy to offer reasons why the thinkers he studies held the opinions they did, to speculate on the premises left tacit in their arguments, to evaluate the coherence and cogency of the inferences they drew. But the supplying of reasons for philosophical conclusions, the detection of hidden premises in philosophical arguments, and the logical evaluation of philosophical inferences are themselves full-blooded philosophical activities. Consequently, essays in the history of philosophy such as this book contains must also be, as I have entitled them in the sub-title, historical essays in philosophy.

The claim that works of philosophy do not date is, of course, a claim which needs qualification. Many branches of philosophy are closely linked to progressive, non-philosophical disciplines and share in the vicissitudes and obsolescence of those disciplines. Thus the philosophy of space and time must mirror the historical development of physics, and the philosophy of logic shares in the evolution and expansion of mathematical logic.

Indeed, it is characteristic of the history of philosophy that philosophical problems are not solved within the confines of philosophy, but generate by fission problems which are soluble by the methods of some non-philosophical discipline. Thus the debates between seventeenth century philosophers about innate ideas have a number of twentieth century heirs only some of which are philosophical while others are decidable by mathematical procedures or experimental research (such as on the one hand the incompletability of arithmetic and on the other the role of heredity vs. environment in concept acquisition). But there are at least two areas in which the boundary between the competence of the *a priori* and *a posteriori* methods of study is so ill drawn that it is dangerous even for an experimental scientist to dismiss the conclusions of the philosophers of the past: I mean the philosophy of mind and the philosophy of language. It is a matter of dispute among philosophers whether this state of affairs is due to the comparative infancy of the sciences of psychology and linguistics, or whether the human mind's ability to reflect on itself and the possibility of self-reference within natural languages entail that the scientific study of language and mind must always leave untouched an irreducibly philosophical residue.

The six essays which constitute the main body of this book are all devoted in different ways to a single fundamental issue in the philosophy of mind: the delimitation and characterization of the different human activities, capacities, faculties which are the elements which constitute mentality. The anatomizing of the parts of the soul is a very ancient philosophical concern, but it is one which cannot be by-passed by the most modern experimental study since it concerns the demarcation of the phenomena to be selected for study. Even a crude operationalism such as finds expression in the slogan 'intelligence is what intelligence tests measure' must take sides on the philosophical issue if it is to regard the different tests as tests of a single thing.

INTRODUCTION ix

The first essay shows how the attempt to assign human activities to different faculties or parts of the soul was begun by Plato: that essay and the third show how he and Aristotle put the notion of parts of the soul with characteristic functions at the service of a half-psychological, half-moral concept of human flourishing or happiness. The second and fifth essays concern the relation between the cognitive and the affective side of human life, between the intellect and the reason on the one hand and the will and the passions on the other: the second essay considers Aristotle's treatment of this problem and the fifth essay Descartes'. The fourth essay concerns the relation between the intellect and the imagination in Aquinas, and the final essay deals with the part played in the identification of mental events in general by consciousness on the one hand and by expression in behaviour on the other. As is clear especially from this last essay, my approach to philosophy of mind has been very strongly influenced by Wittgenstein, but I have tried to get to grips with the texts of the classical philosophers I have discussed and not to treat them, as some admirers of Wittgenstein appear to do, as straw men to be criticized without being quoted.

The paper on the history of the ethics of intention is both in style and content rather different from the other essays and for that reason I have placed it in an appendix. It was originally written as an encyclopedia article and it concerns not only philosophy of mind but also the area in which philosophical psychology overlaps with moral and legal philosophy.

The first essay was originally published in the Proceedings of the British Academy in 1969, the second appeared in *Phronesis* in 1966 and the third in the Proceedings of the Aristotelian Society for 1965–6. I am grateful to the original publishers for permission to reprint these papers in this collection. The fourth, fifth and sixth essays have already appeared in collections, the fourth in *Aquinas, Modern Studies in Philosophy* ed. A. Kenny (Doubleday 1970), the fifth in *Cartesian Studies* ed. R. J. Butler (Blackwell 1972), the sixth in *Wittgenstein, Modern Studies in Philosophy* ed. G. Pitcher (Doubleday 1966).

MENTAL HEALTH IN PLATO'S REPUBLIC

The concept of mental health was Plato's invention. Metaphors drawn from sickness are no doubt as old as metaphor itself, and the first recorded application of the Greek world for 'healthy' was to a sound argument rather than to a sound body (*Iliad* 8. 524). Hebrew and Greek poets used such metaphors on occasion for states of mind, and especially for passion, rage, and madness. Thus Aeschylus' Prometheus is reminded that words are the healers of sick anger (1. 378) and Xerxes' mother in the *Persae* describes the rash ambitions of her son as 'a disease of the mind' (1. 750). The Lord told Isaiah to shut the eyes of his people, lest it be converted and healed (Isa. 6:10) and to Jeremiah he promised to heal the disloyalty of Israel (Jer. 3:21). But nothing in Greek thought before Plato suggests that the notion of a healthy mind was more than a metaphor; and nowhere in the Old Testament is sin represented as a sickness of the soul.[1] It was Plato who, in the *Gorgias* developed the metaphor in unprecedented detail, and in the *Republic* crossed the boundary between metaphor and philosophical theory.

'Bodies and souls', says Socrates in the *Gorgias*, 'can each be in good condition, can they not?'—and he uses the medical term *euexia*. Real *euexia* must be distinguished from apparent *euexia*, though only a doctor or trainer may be able to detect the difference in the case of the body. In the soul, too, there is a condition which counterfeits *euexia*, and there are arts corresponding to the skills of the doctor and the trainer, namely the arts of the lawgiver and the judge. These arts are therapies which minister to what is best in the soul (464a ff.).

Later in the same dialogue we are told that one's property, one's body, and one's soul can all be in an evil state (πονηρία). If

---

[1] See also Sophocles, *Ajax*, 59, 186, 452; Euripides, *Bacchae*, 948; *Orestes*, 10; Liddell and Scott, s.vv. ἰάομαι, ἰατρός, νόσος, ὑγίεια; A. Oepke in Kittel, *Theologisches Wörterbuch zum Neuen Testament*, iv, 1086.

one's property is in a bad state, that is poverty, if one's body is in a bad state, that is disease, and if one's soul is in a bad state that is vice. These three evils may be relieved by the ministrations of three arts: the art of making money, the art of medicine, and the art practised by judges. By now the axe is fully ground, and Plato can administer the blow he has been preparing: to avoid punishment for one's misdeeds, if a judge is like a doctor, is as foolish as to avoid a visit to the surgeon out of fear; except of course that it is worse to live with an unhealthy soul that with an unhealthy body (479c). The allegory is worked out in detail: the pains of judicial punishment are the surgery and cautery of the soul (480b ff.); the desires of an unwell soul should be restrained like the unhealthy appetites of a diseased body (505a). But all this is no more than an allegory, whose point is expressed by Plato in a 'geometric proportion' (465): as medicine is to cookery, so justice is to rhetoric: medicine proves a healthy diet, while cookery flatters taste. The trial of Socrates will be like that of a doctor prosecuted by a cook before a jury of children, who are fonder of sweets than they are of bitter medicine (521d–e). Clearly, all this need not imply that there is literally such a thing as mental health, any more than it implies that there are mental sweetmeats. When Socrates speaks of a healthy soul (479c, 525e, 526d), or of psychic disease (481b, 512b), he need be no more committed to a theory of mental health than an Englishman who speaks of food for thought or mental indigestion is committed to a theory of mental dietetics.

In the *Republic* allegory gives way to theory building. The difference is made by the doctrine of the tripartite soul. The *Republic* is dominated by two quasi-medical ideas: the idea of an organism, and the idea of a function or characteristic activity (ἔργον). The theme of the dialogue is the nature of justice in the state and in the soul; and both state and soul are portrayed as organisms, as complexes of parts with characteristic functions. Justice in state and soul is what health is in the body, namely, the right functioning of the elements of the organism.

There is nothing surprising in the attempt to apply medical concepts to politics and moral psychology. As Jaeger has observed 'the medical art was the only field in which the Greeks of the classical period had arrived at a fairly exact observation and understanding of the processes of nature' (*JHS* 1957 (54), 256). When medicine is the most successful discipline, then the scientific study of the mind or of the state will seem best cast in the medical model. Similarly, Hume, who lived when the most successful science was mechanics, hoped to discover the mechanics of the mind, and offered the principle of association of ideas as the psychic counterpart of gravitation (*Treatise* I. 1. v). Some of the prestige enjoyed in the eighteenth century by the principle of gravitation attached in Plato's time to the doctrine of the balancing of humours.

Alcmaeon had said that health was a balanced constitution (ἰσονομία) of the different powers (δυνάμεις) of which man was made up: wet, hot, dry, cold, sour, sweet (Galen xix. 343, quoted by Jones in the Loeb edition of Hippocrates, p. xlvii). The Hippocratic author of *On Ancient Medicine* (*c.* 420 B.C.) agrees that health is a harmonious mixture or blending of the constituents of man, but regards the humours (phlegm, blood, yellow, and black bile) as more relevant constituents than the philosophical abstractions of hot and cold and wet and dry. Other authors disagreed about the number and nature of the humours, but in all of them, in the words of W. H. S. Jones, 'there is one common principle, that health is a harmonious mingling of the constituents of the body' (ibid., p. 1).

Plato inherited this conception of physical health. In the *Symposium* the physician Eryximachus is able to prove that medicine is under the direction of the god of love, for the doctor 'must be able to reconcile the jarring elements of the body, and force them, as it were, to fall in love with one another. Now we know that the most hostile elements are the opposites—hot and cold, sweet and sour, wet and dry, and so on' (186d). In the *Timaeus* we are told 'There are four natures out of which the body is compacted—earth and fire and water and air—and the unnatural excess or defect of these, or the change of any of them from its own natural place into another . . . or any similar irregularity, produces disorders and diseases' (82b).

Plato's originality was in applying this fashionable theory to the disorders of the soul. To do this he had to locate in the soul elements corresponding to the elements or humours of the body. Once the elements have been located, mental disease can be analysed as a disturbance of the peace between them. Evidences of conflict are not far to seek, and Plato anatomizes the soul in accordance with them. The canonical tripartite division of the soul is described in Book Four, and we will consider that first instead of any of the suggested bipartite divisions to be found elsewhere (e.g. 431a, 602e).

II

Having enumerated the three classes in the State, Guardians, Auxiliaries, and craftsmen, Socrates suggests that the soul too contains three elements (εἴδη).

'Do we', he asks, 'gain knowledge with one part, feel anger with another, and with yet a third desire the pleasures of food, sex, and so on? Or is the whole soul at work in every impulse and in all these forms of behaviour?'[2] To settle the question he appeals to phenomena of mental conflict. A man may be thirsty and yet unwilling to drink; what impels to an action must be distinct from what restrains from it; so there must be one part of the soul which reflects and another which is the vehicle of hunger, thirst, and sexual desire (439d). These two elements can be called reason (τὸ λογιστικόν) and appetite (τὸ ἐπιθυμητικόν). Now anger cannot be attributed to either of these elements; for anger conflicts with appetite (witness Leontius' indignation with himself for his necrophilic desires) and can be divorced from reason (children have tantrums before they reach the years of discretion) (441b). So we must postulate a third element in the soul, temper (τὸ θυμοειδές), to go with reason and appetite.

This division is based on two premises: the principle of non-contrariety, and the identification of the parts of the soul by their desires. If X and Y are contrary relations, nothing can unqualifiedly stand in X and Y to the same thing; and desire and aversion are contrary relations (437b). The desires of appetite are clear enough, and the desires of temper are to fight and punish; but we are not at this point told anything about the desires of reason. No doubt the man in whom reason fights with thirst is one who is under doctor's orders not to drink: in which case the opponent of appetite will be the rational desire for health.

[2] The *Republic* is quoted in Cornford's translation with occasional slight modifications.

In Book Nine we are told more about the desires of the three parts. The lowest can be called the avaricious element, since money is the principal means of satisfying the desires of appetite. Temper seeks power, victory, and repute, and so may be called the honour-loving or ambitious part of the soul. Reason pursues knowledge of truth: its love is learning. In each man's soul one or other of these elements may be dominant: he can be classed accordingly as avaricious, ambitious, or academic (580c–581b).

Looking back, we can see that the three parts of the soul and the three corresponding characters are perceptible from the beginning of the *Republic*. The venerable Cephalus, enthroned in his courtyard, speaks of old age. Many lament it, he says, for they can no longer make love or make merry, and their families show them no respect; but he finds that as bodily pleasures grow dim those of the mind become keener. Old age, that is, leaves appetite unsatisfied, and temper ruffled; but the pleasures of reason are stronger than ever (329a).

Later in Book One, Socrates needs to show that no one is willing to rule without being paid. If a man is to consent to rule 'he must have his recompense in the shape of money or honour, or of punishment in case of refusal'. The three characters are discernible: clearly, the first two rewards are the incentives of the avaricious and ambitious; but the third is not obvious and Glaucon asks for clarification. Socrates explains that this is the recompense of the best type of men, who will only rule for fear of being ruled by their inferiors (347a). This foreshadows the reluctant return of the philosopher kings to watch over the community in the cave (519–21).

Book One also foreshadows the theory that injustice is a falling-out of the elements of the soul. Even thieves cannot prosper without honour among themselves, Socrates reminds Thrasymachus, and in the individual also 'injustice will make him incapable of accomplishing anything because of inner faction and lack of self-agreement, and make him an enemy to himself' (352a). In the final argument with Thrasymachus we are introduced to a concept of psychic flourishing which Plato knows cannot be justified until the investigation of justice has been carried to a deeper level (354b).

The first step to this is the listing of three types of good in Book Two. There are goods chosen for their own sakes without regard to their effects (e.g. harmless fleeting pleasures), goods chosen for their own sakes and for the sake of their effects (understanding, sight, and health) and goods chosen for the sake of their effects only (the art of healing and the making of money). Glaucon places justice in the third class, and Socrates undertakes to show it belongs to the second. Glaucon's position is similar to that of Socrates in the *Gorgias*, for the justice discussed there was judicial punishment, and Socrates' theme was that it was in the criminal's interest to take his medicine (357b–358b).[3]

Describing the ideal state, Socrates has some harsh things to say about doctors. Their presence in the state is a sign that something has gone wrong (405e). It is disgraceful to need a doctor, not for wounds or seasonal infections, but because of sloth and overeating (405c–d). The poor cannot afford to be hypochondriacs, but the rich who have no work to do are encouraged by their doctors to be valetudinarians (407b). How different the practice of Aesculapius: he would cure those capable of returning to civic duties by a brisk treatment of drugs and surgery, 'but treatment, he thought, would be wasted on a man who could not live in his ordinary round of duties and was consequently useless to himself and society' (407d). Plato's admiration for the art of medicine clearly went hand in hand with a contempt for the practice of doctors and a presumption that most patients were malingerers.

In the *Republic* as in the *Gorgias* doctors are compared with judges. But there is a difference between the two. It does not matter if a doctor is himself unhealthy: for doctors do not treat the body with the body, but with the mind. A judge, on the other hand, 'rules soul with soul', and though he must know what injustice is, he must not draw upon his own experience of it in order to diagnose the crimes of others (508e). But in the Ideal State, drastic measures are to be taken to see that the demand for both doctors and judges is strictly limited. 'They will look after those citizens whose bodies and souls are constitutionally sound. The physically unsound they will leave to die; and they will actually put to death those who are incurably corrupt in mind' (410).

Thus far, as in the *Gorgias*, Socrates has been working with a simple contrast between soul and body: what medicine is to

[3] The *Gorgias* analogy is applied from time to time in the discussion of the primary education of the guardians (e.g. 401c; 403c; 405c).

the body, justice is to the soul. But now this simple scheme is complicated. One might think, Socrates says, that gymnastics were for the body, and music (literary and artistic education) for the soul. But no, both are for the soul: gymnastics is to benefit the temper (θυμοειδές), the high-spirited principle, and music for the academic or philosophical nature in us (410d). Excessive gymnastics lead to boorishness; too much music makes effeminate. The purpose of a balanced education is 'to bring the two elements into tune with one another by adjusting the tension of each to the right pitch' (411d). Thus we are introduced to the notion of psychic harmony.

A different bipartition of the soul is made when Socrates discusses expressions such as 'self control' and 'self mastery' as synonyms for temperance. 'The phrase means' he says 'that within the man himself, in his soul, there is a better part and a worse; and that he is his own master when the part which is better by nature has the worse under its control' (431a). These bipartitions are not in conflict with the canonical tripartition of 435: on the contrary, they introduce, in two pairs, the three elements of the later division. The contrast between the two branches of education introduces reason and temper, but does not mention appetite since education is to control, not to develop, appetite. The worse part of the soul which is to be mastered is appetite, (cf. 431c), and reason and temper are lumped together as the better part of the soul just as guardians and auxiliaries, in the same passage, are treated as a single class in the state.

Once the three parts of the soul have been introduced in Book Four the way is open for the identification of justice with mental health. Justice in the state meant that each of the three orders was doing its own proper work (τὰ αὐτοῦ πράττειν—a phrase which can be translated, according to one's political sympathies, either as 'minding one's own business' or 'doing one's own thing'). 'Each one of us likewise will be a just person, fulfilling his proper function, only if the several parts of our nature fulfil theirs' (442a). Reason is to rule, educated temper to be its ally, both are to rule the insatiable appetites and prevent them going beyond bounds. Like justice, the other three cardinal virtues relate to the psychic elements: fortitude will be located in temper, temperance will reside in the unanimity of the three elements, and wisdom will be in 'that small part which rules . . ., possessing as it does the knowledge of what is good for each of the three elements and for all of them in common' (442a–d).

Justice is a prerequisite even for the pursuits of the avaricious and ambitious man. 'Only when a man has linked these parts together in well-tempered harmony and has made himself one man instead of many, will he be ready to go about whatever he may have to do, whether it be making money and satisfying bodily wants, or business transactions, or the affairs of state' (443e). Injustice is a sort of civil strife among the elements, usurping each other's functions. 'Justice is produced in the soul, like health in the body, by establishing the elements concerned in their natural relations of control and subordination, whereas injustice is like disease and means that this natural order is subverted.' The object of the whole exercise is achieved when Glaucon agrees that since virtue is the health of the soul, it is absurd to ask whether it is more profitable to live justly or to do wrong. All the wealth and power in the world cannot make life worth living when the bodily constitution is going to rack and ruin: and can life be worth living when the very principle whereby we live is deranged and corrupted? (445b).

This point established, Socrates goes on to observe that there are as many types of character as there are distinct varieties of political constitution: five of each (445d, cf. 544e). The first and best constitution is called monarchy or aristocracy—if wisdom rules it does not matter whether it is incarnate in one or many rulers. This is described in the long central section on the education of the philosopher king (471c–541). Then Socrates goes on to describe the four other types of character and constitution: timocracy, oligarchy, democracy, and despotism (543c).

Tidy-minded students of Plato sometimes ask: if there are three parts of the soul, why are there four cardinal virtues, and five different characters and constitutions? The second part of this question is easier to answer than the first. There are five constitutions and four virtues because each constitution turns into the next by the downgrading of one of the virtues; and it takes four steps to pass from the first constitution to the fifth. It is when the rulers cease to be men of wisdom that aristocracy gives place to timocracy (547e). The oligarchic rulers differ from the timocrats because they lack fortitude and military virtues (556d). Democracy arises when even the miserly temperance of the oligarchs is abandoned (555b). For Plato, any step from aristocracy is a step away from justice; but it is the step from democracy to despotism that marks the enthronement of injustice incarnate (576a). So the aristocratic state is marked by the presence of all the virtues, the timocratic state by the absence of wisdom, the oligarchic state by the decay of fortitude, the democratic state by contempt for temperance, and the despotic state by the overturning of justice.

But how are these vices and these constitutions related to the parts of the soul? The pattern is ingeniously woven. In the ideal constitution the rulers of the state are ruled by reason, in the timocratic state the rulers are ruled by temper, and in the oligarchic state appetite is enthroned in the rulers' souls (553c). But now within the third part of the tripartite soul a new tripartition appears. The bodily desires which make up appetite are divided into necessary, unnecessary, and lawless desires. Necessary desires are the ones which cannot be got rid of and which do us good to fulfil, like the desires for plain bread and meat. Unnecessary desires are those which can be got rid of by early training, such as a taste for luxuries (559a ff.). Lawless desires are those unnecessary desires which are so impious, perverse, and shameless that they find expression normally only in dreams (571 ff.). The difference between the oligarchic, democratic, and despotic constitutions depends upon the difference between these types of desire. In the oligarchic state a few men rule, in the democratic state the multitude rule, in the despotic state a single man rules. All these rulers are governed by their appetites. The few rulers of the oligarchic state are themselves ruled by a few necessary desires (554a); each of the multitude dominant in the democracy is dominated by a multitude of unnecessary desires (559c); the sole master of the despotic state is himself mastered by a single dominating lawless passion (572e).

Socrates makes further use of the tripartite theory to prove the superiority of the just man's happiness, as promised to Glaucon at 445b. Men may be classified as avaricious, ambitious, or academic according to the dominant element in his soul (579d). Men of each type will claim that their own life is best: the avaricious man will praise the life of business, the ambitious man will praise a political career, and the academic man will praise knowledge and understanding and the life of learning. It is the academic, the philosopher, whose judgement is to be preferred: he has the advantage over the others in experience, insight, and reasoning (582c). Moreover, the objects to which the philosopher devotes his life are so much more real than the objects pursued by the others that their pleasures seem illusory by comparison. The pleasantest, as well as the most virtuous, course for the other elements in the soul is to obey reason. 'All the desires of the ambitious and of the avaricious part of our nature will win the truest pleasures of which they are capable if they accept the guidance of knowledge and reason and pursue only those pleasures which wisdom approves' (587a). Next there follows the famous piece of arithmetical prestidigitation by which Socrates proves that the kingly life of the philosopher is 729 times pleasanter than the life of the passion-ridden tyrant.

At the end of Book Nine we bid farewell to the tripartite soul with a vivid picture. Appetite is a many-headed beast, constantly sprouting heads of tame and wild animals; temper is like a lion; and reason like a man. The beast is larger than the other two, and all three are stowed away within a human being. Injustice starves the man, profligacy feeds fat the monster, ill temper gives too much licence to the lion. 'On the other hand to say that justice pays is to assert that all our words and actions should tend towards giving the man in us complete mastery over the whole human creature, and letting him take the many-headed beast under his care and tame its wildness, like the gardener who trains his cherished plants while he checks the growth of weeds. He should enlist the lion as his ally, and caring for all alike should foster their growth by first reconciling them to one another and to himself' (589b). 'Thus the entire soul, restored to its native soundness will gain, in the temperance and righteousness which wisdom brings, a condition more precious than the strength and beauty which health brings to the body in proportion as the soul itself surpasses the body in worth' (591a).

III

The modern reader of the *Republic* is reminded of another tripartite soul. Freud, towards the end of his life, replaced the dichotomy of conscious and unconscious with a threefold scheme of the mind. 'The mental apparatus', he wrote, 'is composed of an *id* which is the repository of the instinctual impulses, of an *ego* which is the most superficial portion of the id and one which has been modified by the influence of the external world, and of a *superego* which develops out of the id, dominates the ego, and represents the inhibitions of instinct that are characteristic of man' (xx. 266).[4]

Freud's id is very similar to Plato's appetite (ἐπιθυμητικόν). As appetite is the source of the desires for food and sex (437c, 580e), so the id is filled with hunger and love and instinctual drives (xx. 200; xxii. 73). As the monster appetite is much larger than little reason (442c, 580e, 588d), so the id is 'a mental region more extensive, more imposing, more obscure than the ego' (xx. 194). The id is reigned over by the pleasure principle, and knows no morality or judgements of good and evil (xxii. 74); just so, the result of pandering to appetite is that pleasure and pain reign in one's soul instead of law (607a). 'The logical laws of thought', Freud tells us, 'do not apply in the *id*, and this is true above all of the law of contradiction. Contrary impulses exist side by side, without cancelling each other out or diminishing each other' (xxii. 73). So too, because of appetite the soul can be called 'full of diversity and unlikeness and perpetually at variance with itself' (561).

Id differs from appetite in one respect: all that happens in the id is and remains unconscious, while much of appetite is conscious. However, Plato, no less than Freud, thinks that each of us has innate desires of a kind commonly thought shameful, and that these desires, like the instinctual drives of the id, surface only in dreams. 'In sleep the wild beast in us, full-fed with meat or drink, becomes rampant and shakes off sleep to go in quest of what will gratify its own instincts. . . . In phantasy it will not shrink from intercourse with a mother or anyone else, man, god, or brute, or from forbidden food or any deed of blood' (571c). The Oedipal character of the dreams is particularly striking; though of course Freud warns us 'the straightforward dream of sexual relations with one's mother which Jocasta alludes to in the *Oedipus Rex*, is a rarity in comparison with the multiplicity of dreams which psychoanalysis must interpret in the same sense' (xix. 131 ff.).

---
[4] References to Freud are to the Standard Edition of his collected works.

In contrast to the id which contains the passions, the ego, Freud tells us, represents what may be called reason and common sense (XXII. 76). It has much in common with Plato's *logistikon*. Both reason and ego go to sleep at night (XVIII. 109, 57c). Reason is the part of the soul most in touch with what is real, just as the ego is devoted to the reality principle (585c ff.; xx. 194) though of course Plato will not agree with Freud in identifying reality with the external world perceived by the senses. Like reason, the ego has the task of controlling instinctual desires, choosing harmless moments for their satisfaction or diverting their expression (xx. 201). Using the metaphor of the *Phaedrus* Freud compares the ego to a rider and the id to a horse. 'The horse supplies the locomotive energy, while the rider has the privilege of deciding on the goal and of guiding the powerful animal's movement.' But the ego's control is not absolute. It is like a constitutional monarch, without whose sanction no law can be passed, but who hesitates long before imposing his veto on any measure put forward by Parliament (XVIII. 59). Constitutional monarchy found no place among Plato's constitutions, but we are reminded of the oligarchic man whose base desires are only tamed, held down under stress of fear for his fortune (554). But it is the task of psychoanalysis to strengthen the ego's hold on the id (xx, 1. 80), just as it is the task of philosophy to strengthen reason's control over appetite. Freud and Plato use the same metaphors to describe the mechanism of control. Freud speaks in hydraulic terms of the operation of the id as a flow of energy which can find a normal discharge, be channelled into alternative outlets, or be dammed up with disastrous results. So too, when Plato wishes to prove that a life of philosophy will promote temperance, he says 'we surely know that when a man's desires set strongly in one direction, in every other channel they flow more feebly, like a stream diverted into another bed. So when the current has set towards knowledge and all that goes with it, desire will abandon those pleasures of which the body is the instrument and be concerned only with the pleasure which the soul enjoys independently' (485d).

There remains the superego and the temper (θυμοειδές). The superego is introduced as an agency which observes, judges, and punishes the behaviour of the ego, partly identical with the conscience, and concerned for the maintenance of ideals (XXII. 66).

It is strongly personified by Freud, and is described as upbraiding, abusing, and humiliating the ego (XXII. 60); rather as Leontius' temper says to his eyes, when overcome by the morbid desire to stare at the corpses, 'there you are, curse you: feast yourselves on this lovely sight' (440a). Temper and superego are alike in being non-rational, punitive forces in the service of morality, the source of shame and anger with oneself; but they differ also in many ways. Temper is present in children from the start (441a), whereas in young children the part which is later taken on by the superego is played by parental authority (XXII. 62). Moreover, temper is directed as much against others as against oneself, whereas the superego is directed exclusively towards the ego. Some of the superego's functions are ones which Plato would attribute to reason: for instance 'becoming the vehicle of tradition and of all the time-resisting judgements of value which have propagated themselves in this manner from generation to generation' (XXII. 67). However, the superego is, in a way, like the temper in being the source of ambition-fear though not necessarily political ambition. 'The superego is the vehicle of the ego ideal by which the ego measures itself, which it emulates, and whose demand for ever greater perfection it strives to fulfil' (XXII. 65).

Both Freud and Plato regard mental health as harmony between the parts of the soul, and mental illness as unresolved conflict between them. 'So long as the ego and its relations to the id fulfil these ideal conditions (of harmonious control) there will be no neurotic disturbance' (XX. 201). The ego's whole endeavour is 'a reconciliation between its various dependent relationships' (XIX. 149). In the absence of such reconciliation, mental disorders develop: the psychoses are the result of conflicts between the ego and the world, the neuroses in general are the result of conflicts between the ego and the id, and narcissistic neuroses such as melancholia (depression) are the result of conflicts between the id and the superego (XIX. 149 ff.). Plato has no such worked out theory. The four characters other than the aristocratic are not explicitly called illnesses, though the despotic constitution is referred to as 'the fourth and final disease of society' (544c). Moreover, the symptoms of the mental conditions of the timarchic, oligarchic, democratic and despotic men are vicious conduct rather than the eccentricities of the neurotic or the delusions of the psychotic.

Moreover, even in the normal case, the Freudian ego seems to have no such security as reason has in the soul of the philosopher king. At best, it is a servant rather than a master. It serves three tyrannical masters, whose claims are divergent, the external world, the superego and the id. It feels hemmed in on three sides, threatened by three kinds of danger. 'It is observed at every step it takes by the strict superego, which lays down definite standards for its conduct, without taking any account of its difficulties from the direction of the id and the external world, and which, if those standards are not obeyed, punishes it with tense feeling of inferiority and of guilt. Thus the ego, driven by the id, confined by the superego, repulsed by reality, strives to master its . . . task of bringing about harmony among the forces and influences working in and upon it; and we can understand how it is that so often we cannot suppress a cry "Life is not easy" ' (xx. 78).

The reason of the oligarchic man, likewise, is a servant not a ruler. The throne is occupied by appetite. 'He will instal another spirit on the vacant throne, the money-loving spirit of sensual appetite, like the great king with diadem and golden chain and scimitar girt at his side. At its footstool on either side will crouch the two slaves he has forced into subjection: reason and ambition' (553d). We are reminded of a passage from 'The World as Will and Idea' which Freud called 'intensely impressive' and loved to quote. In it Schopenhauer says that it is the joke of life that sex, the chief concern of man, should be pursued in secret. 'In fact', he goes on, 'we see it every moment seat itself, as the true hereditary lord of the world, out of the fullness of its own strength, upon the ancestral throne, and looking down from there with scornful glances, laugh at the preparations which have been made to bind it' (Freud, xix. 221).

IV

The tripartite theory is not Plato's last word in the *Republic* on the nature of the soul, and it is time to take account of the context in which it was first introduced. The *Republic* is dialectical in structure, and we must look at the position which the notion of mental health occupies in the dialectic.

In a well-known passage of Book Six Plato criticizes mathematicians because they start from hypotheses which they treat as obvious and do not feel called upon to give an account of. The dialectician, in contrast, though starting likewise from hypotheses, does not like the mathematician immediately move down from hypotheses to conclusions, but ascends first from hypotheses to an unhypothetical principle, and only then redescends from premise to conclusion. Dialectic 'treats its assumptions, not as first principles, but as hypotheses in the literal sense, things "laid down" like a flight of steps up which it may mount all the way to something that is not hypothetical, the first principle of all; and having grasped this may turn back and, holding on to the consequences which depend upon it, descend at last to a conclusion' (511b). The upward path of dialectic is described again in Book Seven as a course of 'doing away with assumptions and travelling up to the first principle of all, so as to make sure of confirmation there' (533c). The phrase just translated (by Cornford) 'doing away with assumptions' has caused trouble to commentators, who wondered whether τὰς ὑποθέσεις ἀναιροῦσα meant refuting hypotheses or turning them into theorems. The literal meaning of the phrase is surely clear enough: ἀναιρέω, to take up, being the plain opposite of ὑποτίθημι, to lay down. The phrase means 'taking up what has been laid down' or 'unhypothesizing the hypotheses'. What this amounts to, we shall see in a moment. The dialectician is further described as the man who 'demands an account of the essence' (λόγος τῆς οὐσίας) of each thing (534c); and it appears that the unhypothetical principle he ascends to must be the Idea of the Good; for we are told that he must be able to 'separate and distinguish the idea of the good from all else, and persevere through everything in the battle of refutation (διὰ πάντων ἐλέγχων), eager to refute (ἐλέγχειν) in reality and not in appearance, and go through all these things without letting his argument be overthrown' (534bc, trans. Robinson, *Plato's Earlier Dialectic*, 171).

The dialectician operates as follows. He takes a hypothesis, a questionable assumption, and tries to show that it leads to a contradiction. When he reaches a contradiction, he next tests the other premisses used to derive the contradiction, and so on in turn until he reaches a premiss which is unquestionable.

Dialectic is based on eristic, a tournament in which one

contestant defends a thesis which the other contestant attacks by asking questions which must be answered yes or no. The questioner's aim is to get an answer incompatible with the original thesis—this is a refutation, a successful *elenchus*. The defendant's aim is to survive the elenchus with his thesis unrefuted. Eristic, apparently, consisted solely of elenchus and was primarily a training-game in logic; dialectic was a form of search for truth, and did not stop at elenchus but proceeded to the examination of the admissions which led the answerer into the elenchus (cf. Ryle, *Plato's Progress*, 102 ff.).

All this can be illustrated from the first book of the *Republic*; and the illustration will show how the thesis that justice is the health of the soul forms a rung of the dialectical ladder. The first elenchus is very brief. Cephalus puts forward the hypothesis that justice is telling the truth and returning what one has borrowed. Socrates asks: is it just to return a weapon to a mad friend? Cephalus agrees that it is not; and so Socrates concludes 'justice cannot be defined as telling the truth and returning what one has borrowed' (331c–d). Cephalus then withdraws from the debate and goes off to sacrifice.

If this were eristic, that would be the end of the game: fool's mate. But this is dialectic, we are seeking the essence (λόγος τῆς οὐσίας) of justice. So we must examine the further premiss used in deriving the contradiction. The reason why it is unjust to return a weapon to a mad friend is that it cannot be just to harm a friend. So next, Polemarchus, the heir to Cephalus' argument, defends the hypothesis that justice is doing good to one's friends and harm to one's enemies (332b ff.). The refutation of this suggestion takes longer; but finally Polemarchus agrees that it is not just to harm any man at all (335e). The crucial premiss needed for this elenchus is that justice is human excellence (ἀνθρωπεία ἀρετή). It is preposterous, Socrates urges, to think that a just man could exercise his excellence by making others less excellent. Polemarchus is knocked out of the debate because he accepts without a murmur the premiss that justice is human excellence; but Thrasymachus is waiting in the wings to challenge that hypothesis. Justice, he says, is not excellence, but weakness and foolishness, because it is not in the interest of its possessor (338c, 348c). It takes nearly twenty Stephanus pages and some complicated forking procedures to checkmate Thrasymachus; but when he finally agrees that the just man will have a better life than the unjust man, he is driven to agree by a number of concessions he makes to Socrates. For instance, he agrees that the gods are just (353a), that human excellence makes happy (548c), that each thing has a function that it does best (353a), that excellence is doing one's function well (353b), and that the function of the soul is to deliberate, rule, and take care of the person (353d). Given these premises,[5] the elenchus is a fair one, and does not depend, as it seems to at first sight, on a quibbling identification of doing good with doing well. But of course the premises need arguing for, and can all be questioned. Most of them are questioned elsewhere in the Republic: the assumption that the gods are just, for instance, is eloquently challenged by Adeimantus in Book Two (364 ff.).

Each of the definitions debated—that justice is truth-telling and debt-repaying, that justice is human excellence—is a hypothesis. To unhypothesize a hypothesis is to call it in question, whether this results in its being refuted (like the first) or confirmed (like the second).[6] In Book One the dialectical discussion of justice has, of course, only begun. Though the counterhypotheses of the nature of justice have been refuted, and though a correct definition is hinted at in 332c, nothing positive has been established because the elenchi depend on hypotheses which, like the mathematicians', are far from unquestionable. This is made clear by Socrates at the end of the book. 'As long as I do not know what justice is, I am hardly likely to know whether or not it is a virtue, or whether it makes a man happy or unhappy' (354c).

One of the hypotheses assumed against Thrasymachus is that it is the soul's function to deliberate, rule, and take care of the person. This is taken up when the soul is divided into parts in Book Four: these functions belong not to the whole soul but only to reason. In establishing the trichotomy a further assumption is laid down: it is not the case 'that the same thing can ever act or be acted upon in two opposite ways, or be two opposite things, at the same time, in respect of the same part of itself, and

---

[5] Plus some premises, which it would be hazardous to attempt to reconstruct, from the argument about competitiveness (πλεονεκτεῖν) 349b ff.

[6] That justice is human excellence is confirmed by the refutation of the counterthesis that it is foolishness. Book One has no example of a hypothesis being confirmed by surviving an elenchus, because Socrates does not accept Thrasymachus' invitation to become respondent instead of questioner (336c).

in relation to the same object' (437a). Plato makes explicit the provisional nature of the hypothesis. 'As we do not want to spend time in reviewing all . . . objections to make sure that they are unsound, let us proceed on this assumption (ὑποθέμενοι) with the understanding that, if we ever come to think otherwise, all the consequences based on it will fall to the ground' (437a).

This hypothesis seems a harmless one, but in spite of appearances it is far from unquestionable. It is not our principle of contradiction, namely, that it is not the case that both p and not p. Plato is not operating with the notion of propositional negation: he is thinking not of contradictory propositions but of contrary predicates—to be stationary *vs* to be in motion; to be attracted *vs* to be repelled. Moreover, he is not using the post-Fregean notion of predicate as what is left of a sentence if you take out a subject-term such as a proper name. The same 'contrary', for Plato, occurs in '. . . is moving his head' and '. . . is moving his arms'. Hence all the qualifications in his principle of contrariety. A man may be standing still and moving his arms, so if the principle is to hold it must specify that contraries are to apply to the same *part*; a man may be standing at one moment and sitting at the next, so we must specify that the contraries are to apply at the same *time*, and so forth. It seems clear that there is no limit to the number of extra qualifications of this sort which one might have to add to the list in order to make sure that contraries could not hold of the same subject. In fact, Plato believed that it was only of the Ideas or Forms that the principle really holds: everything except Forms is in some way or other qualified by contraries. The Form of Beauty, for instance, neither waxes nor wanes, is not beautiful in one part and ugly in another, nor beautiful at one time and ugly at another, nor beautiful in relation to one thing and ugly in relation to another (*Symposium*, 211a). Whereas all the many beautiful things in the world, as Glaucon admits in Book Five of the *Republic*, 'must inevitably appear to be in some way both beautiful and ugly'. The same is true of all other terrestrial entities, including the soul as described in Book Four: it does not really escape the ubiquity of contrariety. It would take a longer way round, Socrates warns us, to reach the exact truth about the soul (434d).

The longer way round takes us through the Forms to the Idea

of the Good (504b). The tripartite theory of Book Four is only an approximation to the truth because it makes no mention of the theory of Ideas. When these are introduced in Book Five, they are used as the basis of a distinction between two powers (δυνάμεις), knowledge (ἐπιστήμη) and opinion (δόξα). Knowledge concerns the Forms, which alone really are (i.e. for any F, only the form of F is altogether and without qualification F), whereas belief concerns the pedestrian objects which both are and are not (i.e., for any F, anything in the world which is F is also in some respect or other not F). These powers are in turn subdivided in the Line passage of Book Six: opinion includes imagination (εἰκασία) whose objects are 'shadows and reflections' and belief (πίστις) whose objects are 'the living creatures about us and the works of nature or of human hands'. Knowledge *par excellence* is understanding (νόησις) whose method is dialectic and whose object is the realm of Forms. But knowledge also includes thought (διάνοια) whose method is hypothetical, and whose objects are the abstract objects of mathematics, which share with the Forms eternity and unchangeability (like all objects of knowledge they belong to the world of being, not of becoming), and share with terrestrial objects multiplicity (for the geometers' circles, unlike The Circle, can intersect with each other, and the arithmeticians' twos, unlike the one and only Idea of Two, can be added to each other to make four, cf. (525c–526a).[7]

What is the relation between the four segments of the line and the three parts of the soul? Clearly, all segments represent powers or dispositions of the reasoning part of the soul, for they are cognitive states, whereas the other parts of the soul are characterized only by their desires and aversions. Opinion, in Book Five, appears to be the state characteristic not of the avaricious man nor of the ambitious man, but of the counterfeit philosopher, the lover of sights and sounds, the philodoxical man with a passion for theatre and music (487d, 480a, 476b).

Light is thrown on this by the allegory of the Cave, which is intended as an explication of the Line (514a, 517b). The prisoners are chained in the cave, facing shadows of puppets thrown by a fire against the inner wall of the cave. Education in the arts of arithmetic, geometry, astronomy and harmony

[7] I have no space to do more than state brazenly my opinion on a very controverted matter. See Wedberg, *Plato's Philosophy of Mathematics*.

is to release the prisoners from their chains, and to lead them past the puppets and the fire in the shadow-world of becoming, into the open sunlight of the world of being (532). The whole course of education, the conversion from the shadows, is designed for the best part of the soul—i.e. for reason (532c); and the chains from which the pupil must be released if he is to begin his ascent are the desires and pleasures of appetite (519b, cf. 586). The prisoners have already had training in gymnastic and music according to the syllabus of Books Two and Three. Even to start the journey out of the cave you must already be sound of mind and limb (536b).

The education allegorized in the cave then, is the education of the philosopher, not of the avaricious or ambitious man; and the four segments of the Line are the four stages of his intellectual achievement. Plato illustrates the stages most fully in connection with the course in mathematics. The future mathematician, while still a chained prisoner, has had his education in the arts; being as yet a lover of sights and sounds, he will see among the shadows theatrical performances, in which, for instance Palamedes will assist Agammemnon by inventing arithmetic at the siege of Troy. This is imagination (εἰκασία) in mathematics. Once freed from his childish delight in the stage, the pupil will be taught to count and calculate for practical purposes: this will come in useful when as philosopher king he takes his turn as commander-in-chief and has to count his army (525b). (The avaricious man, of course, learns arithmetic only for base money-making purposes 525c.) This is called by Plato dealing with numbers which 'have visible or tangible bodies attached to them': in the allegory, this will be looking at the puppets after turning round from the shadows. Arithmetic properly so called will lead the pupil out of the world of becoming altogether, and teach him to study the abstract numbers which can be multiplied but not changed. In the allegory, these are the reflections in the sunlit water: reflections do not flicker like the shadows cast by the fire-light, but still a single object may have many reflections (516a). This is thought (διάνοια) just as the counting of bodies was belief (πίστις). Finally, dialectic, by questioning the hypotheses of arithmetic—researching, as we should say, into the foundations of mathematics—will give him true understanding (νόησις) of number, by introducing him to the Forms

MENTAL HEALTH IN PLATO'S REPUBLIC

in their dependence on the Idea of Good. These Forms are the men and trees and stars and sun of the allegory (516b).

The *Republic* is concerned less with mathematical education than with moral education: but this follows a parallel path. Imagination in morals consists of the dicta of poets and tragedians (331e etc.). If the pupil has been educated in the bowdlerized literature recommended by Plato, he will have seen justice triumphing on the stage, and will have learnt that the gods are unchanging, good, and truthful (382e). This he will later see as a symbolic representation of the eternal Idea of Good, source of truth and knowledge. The first stage of moral education will make him competent in the human justice which operates in law-courts (517d). This will give him true belief: but it will be the task of dialectic to teach him the real nature of justice and to display its participation in the Idea of the Good.[8] It is the first stages of this dialectic that are represented for us in the *Republic* from Books One to Six.

At the end of the upward path of dialectic is the Idea of the Good (505a). A philosopher who had contemplated that idea would no doubt be able to replace the hypothetical definition of justice as psychic health with a better definition which would show beyond question the mode of its participation in goodness (504b). But as he approaches the summit of the mount of dialectic to learn from goodness itself the first principles of law and morality, Socrates, like Moses, disappears into a cloud. He can talk only in metaphor, and cannot give even a provisional account of goodness itself (506d). When next we see clearly, dialectic has begun its downward path. We return to the topics of the earlier books—the natural history of the state, the divisions of the soul, the happiness of the just, the deficiencies of poetry— but we study them now in the light of the theory of Forms. The just man is happier than the unjust, not only because his soul is in concord, but because it is more delightful to fill the soul with understanding than to feed fat the desires of appetite. Reason is no longer the faculty which takes care of the person, it is akin to the unchanging and immortal world of truth (585c). And the poets fall short, not just because they spread unedifying stories

---

[8] In moral education there is no stage corresponding to initiation into the mathematical objects: that is why mathematics is a uniquely valuable propaedeutic for dialectic (531d).

and pander to effeminate tastes, but because they operate at the third remove from the reality of the Forms (595a–602b).

In Book Ten Plato returns for the last time to the anatomy of the soul. The tripartite division of the earlier books is recalled in the first lines, but the divisions actually made in the book are all bipartite. Thus, there is one element in the soul which is confused by bent-looking sticks in water, and another element which measures, counts, and weighs. The latter is called λογιστικόν which is the word used for reason in Book Four. But it does not appear that the parts here contrasted are two out of the earlier triad. Rather, the contrast recalls the difference between imagination (whose objects included reflections in water) and belief (which deals with measurement and the numbers attached to visible bodies 526d). It is a contrast between two elements within the single realm of reason in the tripartite soul.[9]

In the actions represented by drama, Plato continues, there is an internal conflict in a man analogous to the conflict between the contrary opinions induced by visual impressions (603d). In tragedy, this conflict is between a lamentation-loving part of the soul (θρηνωδές 606a, ἀγανακτητικόν 604e) and the best part of us which is willing to abide by the law which says we must bear misfortune quietly (604b). In comedy this noble element has to fight with another element which has an instinctive impulse to play the clown (606c). It is no doubt futile to ask whether these elements in the soul are to be identified with any yet mentioned. Perhaps the tragic and comic elements take their place along with appetite and temper as potential foes to reason. Certainly at 608b poetry appears along with wealth and honour as an ambition which might distract one from the pursuit of justice: the three competing lives appear to have been joined by a fourth.

The notion of mental health makes its final appearance in the proof of immortality which concludes Book Ten. Each thing is destroyed by its characteristic disease (κακία): eyes by ophthalmia, and iron by rust. Now vice is the characteristic disease of the soul; but vice does not destroy the soul in the way disease destroys the body (609d). But if the soul is not killed by its own disease, it will hardly be killed by diseases of anything else—

---

[9] This is confirmed by the use made at 602e of the principle of contrariety: 'it is impossible for the same part of the soul to hold two contrary beliefs at the same time'. Earlier, it was desires which were contrasted.

certainly not by bodily disease—and so it must be immortal.

The principle that justice is the soul's health is now finally severed from the tripartite theory of the soul on which it rested. An uneasily composite entity like the threefold soul, Socrates says, could hardly be everlasting. The soul in its real nature is a far lovelier thing in which justice is much more easily to be distinguished. Our description of the soul, says Socrates, is true of its appearance; but it is now afflicted by many evils, and more like a monster than its natural self, like a statue of a sea-god covered by barnacles. If we could fix our eyes on the soul's love of wisdom and passion for the divine and everlasting, we would realize how different it would be freed from the pursuit of earthly happiness. Whether the soul thus seen in its true nature would prove manifold or simple is left an open question (611b ff.).

V

The title of this paper may well seem to contain an equivocation. By now it is abundantly clear that Plato's conception of the health of the soul is fundamentally a moral concept, so that it is surely misleading to render it by the medical notion of mental health. This is not so. Plato was deliberately assimilating a moral concept to a medical one, and the contemporary concept of mental health has a moral as well as a medical component.

By defining justice as the health of the soul Plato achieved three things. First, he provided himself with an easy answer to the question 'why be just?' Everyone wants to be healthy, so if justice is health, everyone must really want to be just. If some do not want to behave justly, this can only be because they do not understand the nature of justice and injustice and lack insight into their own condition. Thus the doctrine that justice is mental health rides well with the Socratic theses that no one does wrong voluntarily, and that vice is fundamentally ignorance. Secondly, if injustice is a disease, it should be possible to eradicate it by the application of medical science. So Plato can offer the strict training programme and educational system of the *Republic* as the best preventative against an epidemic of vice. Thirdly, if every vicious man is really a sick man, then the virtuous philosopher can claim over him the type of control which a doctor has over his patients. To treat injustice as mental sickness is to assimilate vice to madness, as Plato often does explicitly (e.g. 329d). The point is made very early on in the *Republic* that madmen have no rights: they may not claim their property, they are not entitled to the truth (331c). But of course, by Plato's standards, all who fall short of the standards of the philosopher king are more or less mad: and thus the guardians are allowed to use the 'drug of falsehood' on their subjects (382c). The thesis that madmen need restraint is harmless only so long as it is not combined with the view that all the world is mad but me and possibly thee.

In our own day those who share a Platonic enthusiasm for the replacement of judges by doctors share some of these features of Plato's outlook. An understandable reluctance to pass moral judgements and a well-founded distrust of retributivist theories of punishment inclines many people to welcome the suggestion that all criminals are sick rather than vicious people. The suggestion is made even more attractive by the corollary that it may be possible to eradicate crime by the application of medical science. The humane and benevolent optimism characteristic of this approach is not incompatible with a certain ruthlessness in its practical application. For while we await the growth of insight in the patients and the progress of research among the doctors, the *ci-devant* criminals have to be restrained pretty much as before. But the safeguards against unjustified restraint do not have to be as rigorous as heretofore. Obviously, the standards of evidence required to show that someone is a patient requiring treatment do not have to be as rigid as those required to show that he is a guilty man meet for punishment.

These Platonic features, it seems to me, are detectable in the Mental Health Act of 1959, which introduced into English law the concept of the psychopath. 'Psychopathic disorder' is defined in the Act as 'a persistent disorder or disability of mind (whether or not including subnormality of intelligence) which results in abnormally aggressive or seriously irresponsible conduct on the part of the patient, and requires, or is susceptible to medical treatment'. The extremely broad nature of this definition was frequently remarked in the Parliamentary debates which preceded its enactment (e.g. by Lord Silkin, Lords Debates, 7 May 1959). It is clear that the diagnosis of this condition in effect calls for a moral judgement as to the limits of normal aggressiveness and the boundary between frivolity and serious irresponsibility. Lady Wootton remarked perceptively in the House of Lords that the act marked a landmark in 'a social development characteristic of the age—the encroachment of the science of medicine on the province formerly reserved for morals'. (Lords Debates, 4 June 1959). Whether or not, as Lady Wootton believed, every recidivist is *eo ipso* a psychopath by this definition, it is certain that the symptoms of psychopathic disorders to be found in textbooks remind one forcibly of Plato's description of the democratic man. Psychopathic disorder is, indeed, as much of a moral concept as a medical one. Medical authorities disagree about the nature, and indeed the very existence, of a psychopathic syndrome. The provision of the Act that the psychopath must 'require, or be susceptible to, medical treatment' is insufficient to constitute a genuine medical category. All anti-social behaviour 'requires medical treatment' in the minimal sense that it would be convenient if a drug could be found to put a stop to it. In this section, the Act appears to be, like Plato, redescribing moral phenomena in medical terms. And the Platonic corollaries follow. The Act of 1959 made it easier, not harder, for a man to be detained against his will, provided that the detention was not in prison but in a hospital.

The modern development of the concept of mental health dates from the end of the nineteenth century when Freud, Charcot, and Breuer began to treat hysterical patients as genuine invalids instead of malingerers. This, it has often been said, was as much a moral decision as a medical discovery. But most of us would feel that it was the right moral decision: and hysteria is close enough to the paradigm of physical illness for the concept of mental illness to have clear sense when applied to it. In the paradigmatic cases of illness the causes, symptoms, and remedies of disease are all physical. In the paradigmatic cases of mental illness (e.g. schizophrenia) organic causes are known or suspected and treatment by physical methods (drugs, electroconvulsive therapy) is at least partially effective. What makes such illnesses *mental* illnesses is that the symptoms concern the cognitive and affective life of the patient: disorders of perception, belief, and emotion. In the diagnosis of whether perception is normal, of whether belief is rational, of whether emotion is out of proportion, there is a gentle slope which leads from clinical description to moral evaluation. Still, in such cases, even when diagnosis is as it were infected with morality, the relation to organic cause and physical treatment is strong enough to give clear content to the concept of disease. About such diseases—which include many which would have been recognized even in Plato's time as madness—much has been learnt in the present century, largely through the work of the psychiatrists whom Freud despised as much as Plato despised the Athenian doctors of his time. But as a result of the popularization of Freudian ideas the concept of mental health and sickness has been moralistically broadened just as it was by Plato: and Freudian theory has provided no better scientific justification of this broadening than did Plato's tripartite theory of the soul which in part it resembles. If a psychopath is given psychotherapy, we have a case in which neither the alleged causes of the condition (e.g. a broken home), nor its symptoms (e.g. petty theft), nor its cure (e.g. group discussions) have anything in common with the causes, symptoms, or cure of organic diseases. In such a case, the concept of mental illness has become a mere metaphor; and whatever value these procedures may have must be capable of commendation by something other than metaphor.

It is characteristic of our age to endeavour to replace virtues by technology. That is to say, wherever possible we strive to use methods of physical or social engineering to achieve goals which our ancestors thought attainable only by the training of character. Thus, we try so far as possible to make contraception take the place of chastity, and anaesthetics to take the place of fortitude; we replace resignation by insurance policies and munificence by the Welfare state. It would be idle romanticism to deny that such techniques and institutions are often less painful and more efficient methods of achieving the goods and preventing the evils which unaided virtue once sought to achieve and avoid. But it would be an equal and opposite folly to hope that the take-over of virtue by technology may one day be complete, so that the necessity for the laborious acquisition of the capacity for rational choice by individuals can be replaced by the painless application of the fruits of scientific discovery over the whole field of human intercourse and enterprise. The moralistic concept of mental health incorporates the technological dream: it looks towards the day when virtue is superseded by medical know-how. But we are no more able than Plato was to make ourselves virtuous by prescription or pharmacology: and renaming virtue 'mental health' takes us no further than it took Plato in the direction of that chimeric goal.

THE PRACTICAL SYLLOGISM AND INCONTINENCE[1]

Philosophers do not agree whether a man can voluntarily do what he believes to be wrong. This disagreement has coloured their opinions of Aristotle's treatment of incontinence in the seventh book of the *Nicomachean Ethics*. Some, believing that one cannot—unless prevented—fail to do what one believes to be the best thing to do at the moment of action, have praised Aristotle for sharing the same belief. Others, holding a different opinion, have regretted that Aristotle in this passage misrepresents the moral struggle. They have consoled themselves by alleging other texts in a contrary sense. Thus, Sir David Ross: 'Aristotle elsewhere shows himself alive to the existence of a moral struggle, a conflict between rational wish and appetite, in which the agent has actual knowledge of the wrongness of the particular act that he does. We must suppose that interest in his favourite distinctions of potential and actual, of major and minor premise, has betrayed him into a formal theory which is inadequate to his own real view of the problem. What is missing in his formal theory is the recognition that incontinence is due not to failure of knowledge, but to weakness of will.' (*Aristotle*, 224).

I wish to argue that both the praise and the blame thus accorded to Aristotle are unwarranted. I shall try to show that in the central passage of Chapter Three (1147a24 ff.), Aristotle expressly provides for the case 'in which the agent has actual knowledge of the wrongness of the particular act that he does'. Failure to recognize this, I shall contend, is due to misunderstanding of the structure of the practical syllogism.

Aristotle's starting-point is the popular notion of incontinence

---

[1] A draft of this paper was read at the Philosophical Society in Oxford. I am indebted to the members of the Society, and in particular to Mr. R. M. Hare, for their helpful criticism.

THE PRACTICAL SYLLOGISM AND INCONTINENCE 29

set out in the first two chapters. The incontinent man (ἀκρατής) properly so called, the one who merits the title without qualification, is a man who pursues pleasure (1146a32, b24), pleasures of touch and taste in food and drink and sex (1118a26 ff.). He is overcome by pleasure; yet he acts, it seems, willingly: for it is argued that a man cannot be wise (φρόνιμος) and incontinent at the same time, on the grounds that no-one would say that it was characteristic of the wise man to do evil willingly (1145b35, 1146a7). He does not, however, act on principle or out of considered choice; he does not believe that the thing to do is always to pursue the present pleasure (1146b23). He is contrasted with the intemperate man (ἀκόλαστος), who acts out of conviction and considered choice (1146a32). The incontinent man does not stick to his reasoning (1145b12): through passion he does what he knows to be wrong (εἰδὼς ὅτι φαῦλα πράττει διὰ πάθος 1145b12). Incontinence is something evil and blameworthy (1145b10).

We cannot assume that Aristotle himself would necessarily endorse every detail of the popular concept of incontinence: but that is where he starts from. Moreover, most of the details are reaffirmed after Aristotle's own analysis of the concept. The incontinent *sans phrase* pursues the excessive and unreasonable bodily pleasures of the intemperate, not by considered choice but against his better judgement (1148a7, 17; 1151a7, 11). He is conquered by desire (1149b2), pleasures (1150a13, b7, 25), passion (1151a2); but he acts willingly for in a way he knows what he is doing and why (1152a15; cf. E.E.1224a8 ff.). He is overcome by passion to the extent that he acts against the ὀρθὸς λόγος, but not to the extent that he believes that he ought to pursue such pleasures without reserve; his principles are uncorrupted (1151a 21). One form of incontinence consists in failing to stick to one's reasoning (1150b20). The incontinent man is conscious of his incontinence (1150b31). Incontinence is not only undesirable but blameworthy (1148b6); not just as a fault but as a kind of vice (ὡς κακία τις) (1148a3): not precisely κακία (1150b35, 1151a5), πονηρία rather than μοχθηρία (1150b30-35), indeed the incontinent is not strictly even πονηρός, but just ἡμιπόνηρος (1152a17).

Aristotle's first and principal problem is this: how can a man be incontinent in action while making a correct judgement? (1145b22). If an agent has knowledge, must not his knowledge dominate his action? Socrates said that incontinence as popularly conceived was impossible. If someone judges that it is best to act thus and so, he cannot act otherwise; if he acts otherwise it must be that he does not know what is best. Socrates' theory is in clear contradiction to common sense: so the state of the incontinent needs investigation. If he acts through ignorance, then it must be a special kind of ignorance. ὅτι γὰρ οὐκ οἴεται, he says, ὁ ἀκρατευόμενος πρὶν ἐν τῷ πάθει γενέσθαι, φανερόν.

What does οὐκ οἴεται mean in this cryptic remark? Clearly, what the incontinent man is supposed to be doing if he οὐκ οἴεται is the same as what he is supposed to be doing if he ἀγνοεῖ. Both verbs signify the same faulty state of mind concerning the morality of the action: at least before the onset of passion the incontinent lacks this faulty state of mind. ἄγνοια, then, is not just ignorance: it is positively mistaken belief. This is common enough in Aristotle: at Topics 148a8 he even says that ἄγνοια is never merely non-possession of knowledge, else infants would have it. [2]

The faulty state of mind in the present case is given by 1146b23, 1151a23: it is the belief that one should pursue the present pleasure. The state of mind of the incontinent before the onset of passion is defined by contrast to this. The intemperate man νομίζει ἀεὶ δεῖν τὸ παρὸν ἡδὺ διώκειν; the incontinent οὐκ οἴεται.

Unfortunately, there is here a quadruple ambiguity. There is a difference between

(1) It is not the case that he thinks that p.

(2) He thinks that it is not the case that p.

(1), not (2), is compatible with his having no belief either way about p. Both (1) and (2) could be represented in Greek by οὐκ οἴεται p.

Secondly, there is a difference between

(3) It is not the case that one ought to φ.

(4) It is the case that one ought not to φ.

(3), not (4), is compatible with φ-ing being an indifferent action. Both (3) and (4) could be represented in Greek by οὐ δεῖ φ.

Thirdly, there is a difference between

(5) One ought not to pursue everything A.

(6) Whatever is A ought not to be pursued.

(5), not (6), permits the pursuit of a few things which are A. (5) and (6) can both be represented by the same Greek expression, e.g. οὐ δεῖ διώκειν πᾶν τὸ A.

[2] I am indebted for this reference to Prof. G. Ryle.

Fourthly, 'Always pursue the present pleasure' may mean
(7) Always pursue pleasure of the kind now present, or
(8) Whatever pleasure presents itself, pursue it.
(7) and (8) may both be represented by the Greek ἀεὶ δεῖν τὸ παρὸν ἡδὺ διώκειν.

As a result of these ambiguities, there are nine possible non-equivalent translations of the two words οὐκ οἴεται.
(a) He does not think he must pursue every pleasure
(b) He thinks it is not the case that he must pursue every pleasure
(c) He thinks he must not pursue every pleasure
(d) He does not think he must pursue any pleasure
(e) He thinks it is not the case that he must pursue any pleasure
(f) He thinks he must not pursue any pleasure
(g) He does not think he must pursue this kind of pleasure
(h) He thinks it is not the case that he must pursue this kind of pleasure
(i) He thinks he must not pursue this kind of pleasure.

It is not clear which of these Aristotle had in mind. Indeed, it seems likely, as I shall later argue, that he did not clearly distinguish between them all.

Having used ἄγνοια in the strong sense of *mistaken belief* Aristotle surprisingly goes on to consider the weak sense of *correct belief falling short of knowledge*. There are those, he says, who solve the Socratic problem by saying that in incontinence it is not knowledge, but only belief, which is overcome by pleasure: the incontinent does not really know, but only believes, that he had best not do what he does; his judgement is not firm but hesitant. Thus, Socrates' position is saved—nothing can overcome knowledge—yet we save the phenomena also: the incontinent genuinely does what he believes wrong (1145b31 ff.).

Aristotle is dissatisfied with this solution, and later argues convincingly against it (1146b24 ff.). But first he produces a very puzzling counter-argument. Indeed, it is not altogether clear whether the lines which follow (1145b36 ff.) are a continuation of the thesis of the τινές, or a refutation of it. If the former, the argument must run as follows. If the judgement which opposes the action is not strong but hesitant, then the incontinent man can be excused for giving it up in face of strong desire. This is what distinguishes incontinence from intemperance: incontinence is excusable, but intemperance, like other forms of μοχθηρία is not. Such an argument would involve the conclusion that incontinence was involuntary, for only involuntary acts deserve συγγνώμη (1109b32).

The structure of the passage, and the parallel in the *Magna Moralia* (1200b38) make it more probable that this is a *modus tollens* in Aristotle's own person. If the judgement of the incontinent man were not strong but hesitant, then he would indeed be excusable; but in fact he is not excusable, for incontinence, like μοχθηρία, is blameworthy (1145a16, b10); *ergo* it is not just a hesitant opinion which the incontinent man acts counter to. There arise two difficulties. If this is what Aristotle meant, it would have been simpler if he had said: τῇ δ'ἀκρασίᾳ οὐ συγγνώμη instead of τῇ δὲ μοχθηρίᾳ οὐ συγγνώμῃ,, οὐδὲ τῶν ἄλλων οὐδενὶ τῶν ψεκτῶν. Moreover, if the incontinent can be excused because he is not sure that what he does is wrong, surely, *a fortiori*, the intemperate can be excused because he is sure that what he does is not wrong. But mistaken beliefs about what one ought to do deserve not excuse but blame, as Aristotle says emphatically (1110b28, 1111a1).[3]

The later argument, though not entirely clear, raises less difficulty.[4] It will not do, we are told at 1146b27 ff., to argue that acting against belief is less paradoxical than acting against knowledge. For it is not always that belief is a less firm commitment than knowledge. Some people cling as firmly to their beliefs as others to their knowledge: especially those who believe that their opinions are in fact knowledge. Cf. Heraclitus.

We may agree that belief, unlike knowledge, is compatible with hesitation. If I am right in claiming to know that *p*, then I have the right to refuse to be talked out of believing that *p*. If I merely believe that *p*, I have no such right. But Aristotle says correctly that belief, especially if mistaken for knowledge by its possessor, *may* be, though it *need* not be, just as tough a state of

---

[3] The first difficulty was noticed by Grosseteste (quoted in Walter Burleigh's *Expositio super X libros Ethicorum*). The second was discussed by Ramsauer; Gauthier and Jolif solve it by treating the argument as *ad hominem*.
[4] The relationship of the two arguments is not clear. Aquinas, in his commentary, regards them as complementary. If the incontinent has not knowledge but opinion his opinion is either weak or firm; if weak, then his incontinence is excusable; if firm, then his incontinence is as paradoxical as if he had knowledge.

mind as knowledge. In such a case there may remain at least two possible differences between belief and knowledge. Belief, unlike knowledge, can be false (1139b18); and a belief, even if correct, may be insufficiently grounded for knowledge (1139b33). It is not clear which of these cases Aristotle has in mind: it might be clearer if we knew whether Heraclitus was being cited as an instance or as an authority.[5] The reference to 'those who think they know' suggests a case in which the beliefs are false; but this would be inapposite to the context, for the beliefs of the incontinent are not false.

Perhaps, then, Aristotle is thinking of a case where belief is a firm adhesion, and a correct one, but falls short of knowledge by not being sufficiently grounded. Notoriously, Aristotle had excessively high standards for the sufficiency of grounds for ἐπιστήμη: nothing was really an object of knowledge unless it was a general proposition capable of syllogistic deduction from self-evident principles (*An. Post.* 71. b20 ff.). But this official doctrine is not much in evidence in this context—though even here, I shall argue, Aristotle tries to avoid using ἐπιστήμη for knowledge of particulars. The relevant distinction here appears to be that between the genuine σπουδαῖος who really knows moral truths, and the young pupil who has still to take them on trust (1147a21; 1095a1 ff.). A youth who had had a good education might become incontinent; he would retain the good principles imparted to him, despite his evil actions; but these principles in him are mere opinions, since he lacks the experience which would have grounded them as knowledge. Even in such a case incontinence sets a problem: for though knowledge is lacking, it is not in virtue of any hesitancy of judgement that the agent's state of mind differs from knowledge. So the ἐπιστήμη/δόξα distinction is rejected as a principle of solution.

Others are suggested at 1146b31 ff. What follows breaks into four main sections, up to 1147b5. Opinions differ whether Aristotle is presenting several solutions of one problem (Burnet), several solutions of several problems (Stewart), or one solution in several stages (Gauthier and Jolif). Many commentators, notably Cook Wilson, have divided and emended the text. Certainly our text is not in perfect order: but it appears a merit

---

[5] Instance: Burnet, Grant, Joachim and all medieval commentators following M. M. 1201 b8; authority: Gauthier and Jolif, following Deichgräber.

of the interpretation I shall propose that it requires a minimum of textual adaptation.

At 1146b31, a distinction is drawn between the possession and exercise of knowledge. It seems clear that 'to use knowledge' in line 32 is equivalent to θεωρεῖν in lines 33–5; so too 'use' in 47a2, a12. In 46b32, 47a1–2, 47a12 'using' is contrasted with 'having'; in 47a7 ἔχειν is contrasted with ἐνεργεῖν, a verb which also appears in 47a32, perhaps in contrast with ἔνεστιν, perhaps again in contrast with ἔχειν. With these three pairs of expressions Aristotle is making a single contrast. Two cases are possible: (1) a man may have the knowledge that p, the knowledge that p is in him; (2) he exercises the knowledge that p, the proposition that p 'operates' in him, he 'contemplates' it. Wherever there is (2) there is (1), but not vice versa.

What is it to exercise the knowledge that p? Is it to act upon the knowledge that p? Or is it simply to have the thought that p in one's consciousness? The Greek commentators took the latter view. It is not surprising, they say, if a geometer, while chatting, fails to notice a mistake in a diagram; or if a grammarian, while thinking of something else, gives a wrong answer to a question about the length of a syllable (*Heliodorus E. N. Paraphr., Comm. in Ar. Graeca*, xix, II, 140). Albertus Magnus took the former view. The mere possession of knowledge, for him, includes the case of thinking about it—that is like looking at pictures of delights upon a wall. Exercising knowledge means acting on it: *uti scientia in agere, ita scilicet quod sit principium actionis*.

Either alternative, it seems to me, leads to difficulty. The distinction between knowing and thinking about what one knows is not what we are looking for in this context. The distracted geometer, once his mistake is pointed out to him, will correct it. If the incontinent is in a similar state of mind, then in order to convert him from his misconduct, it would be sufficient to point out that, as he knows, he ought not to be acting as he does. And this surely ἀμφισβητεῖ τοῖς φαινομένοις ἐναργῶς. The incontinent man does not fornicate inadvertently.

On the other hand, we cannot take 'use' simply to mean 'act upon'. In the most obvious sense of 'act upon', a man cannot act upon his knowledge of what he ought to do and yet not do what he ought. But of course, to observe that men do not act upon all their beliefs is to set, not to solve, the problem of incontinence.

THE PRACTICAL SYLLOGISM AND INCONTINENCE 35

In particular it is not to solve the Socratic problem: for if something comes between ἐπιστήμη and its exercise, is not ἐπιστήμη being treated like a slave? We must look, therefore, further into the contrast between the possession and the exercise of knowledge. In the aviary passage of the *Theaetetus*, Plato draws a distinction between the possessing (κεκτῆσθαι) and the holding (ἔχειν) of pieces of knowledge. Every piece of knowledge we have is a bird in our aviary; but only one bird at a time is in our hand. For instance, a mathematician has in his possession a great deal of information about numbers, but when he is counting he needs to grasp individual items of knowledge, as a man catches a bird in his hand. So too with a man who knows his letters, when he is reading. 'You possessed the knowledge for some time, but did not have it handy in your mind' (197–8).

Plato's distinction is echoed in many places by Aristotle. In the *De Anima* (417a26 ff.) he distinguishes between the ἔχων τὴν γραμματικήν who is βουληθεὶς δυνατὸς θεωρεῖν ἂν μή τι κωλύσῃ τῶν ἔξωθεν and the man who is ἤδη θεωρῶν ἐντελεχείᾳ ὢν καὶ κυρίως ἐπιστάμενος τόδε τὸ Α. The grammarian, he says, is a knower in potency, but not like a man who has yet to learn his letters: he undergoes a quite different change, ἐκ τοῦ ἔχειν τὴν γραμματικήν, μὴ ἐνεργεῖν δέ, εἰς τὸ ἐνεργεῖν.[6]

These passages suggest as a translation of θεωρεῖν 'to apply knowledge to a particular instance'. The grammarian knows that every 'A' is to be pronounced A, the arithmetician, that $7+5=12$. They exercise their knowledge when they realize that this 'A' is to be pronounced A, that these seven books and these five books make twelve books. It is not a case of simply calling to mind in an idle moment of reflection that 'A' is pronounced A, or that $7+5=12$.[7]

We might therefore take Aristotle to be arguing as follows. The incontinent man knows in general that his type of behaviour is wrong; but he doesn't apply this knowledge to the particular

---

[6] That Aristotle has the *Theaetetus* in mind is suggested by his argument that a grammarian calling knowledge to mind is not *learning*. Similar distinctions are made elsewhere in the Aristotelian corpus: 130a21, 412a10, 429b8, 1017b4 etc.

[7] In the Aristotelian passages outside the present context, the contrast seems to be between a geometer at work and a geometer not doing geometry at all; not—as in the paraphrast—between a geometer working with his mind on his work and a geometer with his mind elsewhere.

instance; he doesn't realize that what he is actually doing is wrong. But if we do this, is not the next sentence—ἔτι ἐπεὶ 1146b35— very puzzling? If to use a general principle is to apply it to a particular instance, it does not seem possible for the general premiss to be used while the particular premiss is not. For, on this view, the use of the general premiss is precisely the recognition of the instance as falling under it: and is it not just this which the particular premiss verbalizes?

Moreover, if the knowledge of the premisses is not followed by action, how does one know that it is the particular premiss which is unexercised and not the universal?

The answer to these questions must be sought in the nature of the practical syllogism. In the *De Anima*, the *De Motu Animalium*, and the *N. Ethics*, Aristotle gives about ten different examples of such syllogisms. Scarcely any two of them are wholly alike in structure: but the kind that has become most popular, perhaps because it is fairly simple, is that illustrated in 1147a29: 'everything sweet is to be tasted, and this is sweet'—leading to tasting this. When, therefore, in these lines 1147a1 f. we read that there are two kinds of premisses, one universal and the other κατὰ μέρος, it is natural to take the κατὰ μέρος premiss as being a singular proposition, like 'this is sweet'. But a very cursory acquaintance with the *Prior Analytics* reveals that κατὰ μέρος commonly means not a singular, but a particular proposition. (Cf. e.g. 24a17-20, 25a5, 20, 26a30, 33, and *passim*). But, more to the point, the πρότασις κατὰ μέρος can in fact be a universal proposition, provided only that its subject is of lesser extension than the universal which is the subject of the καθόλον. This is made clear by a passage in the *Posterior Analytics* which deserves to be quoted at length.

'The clearest indication that universal demonstration is more authoritative is that when we comprehend the former of the two premisses we have knowledge in a sense of the latter as well, and comprehend it potentially. E.g., if anyone knows that every triangle has the sum of its interior angles equal to two right angles, he knows in a sense also (viz., potentially) that the sum of the interior angles of an isosceles triangle is equal to two right angles, even if he does not know that the isosceles is a triangle. But the man who comprehends the latter premiss does not in any sense know the universal fact, neither potentially nor actually. Moreover universal demonstration is intelligible, whereas particular demonstration terminates in sense perception.'

If we interpret our present passage on the model of this, we must say that the sort of syllogism Aristotle has in mind is not 'Adultery is to be avoided, this is adultery, so . . .'. Rather, it is: 'Injustice is to be avoided; adultery is unjust, so . . .'. And if this is the correct interpretation, we can see how the universal premiss can operate without the particular premiss operating. The exercise of the universal premiss is, for instance, the recognition of the need to avoid adultery—the drawing of the conclusion from the two premisses above. This is compatible with a failure of operation on the part of the particular premiss, viz., the failure to recognize *this*, that I am about to do, as adultery (perhaps because of self-deceit, special pleading, or culpable failure to inquire). This failure is sufficient to inhibit action in accordance with the universal moral principle: πρακτὰ γὰρ τὰ καθ' ἕκαστα.

That this is the correct interpretation is suggested by the immediately following sentence—which is a development of the same argument, not a new one (no 'ἔτι'). The practical syllogism we are given at 1147a5 is not the simple type beloved of commentators but contains no less than four atomic premisses: two, on the face of it, universal and two singular. It runs, in Bywater's text, 'Dry food suits every man, I am a man, such and such food is dry, this is such and such, so . . .'.[8] But Aristotle constantly talks as if there were only *two* premisses in a practical syllogism (e.g. 1147a1, a25). If we are to take this seriously in the present case, we must take either the major or the minor premiss to be composite. Since 'such and such food is dry' appears to be a universal proposition, and since only 'this is such-and-such' is said to be ineffective in a context in which we are discussing the effectiveness of the universal and the ineffectiveness of the particular, we might be tempted to take 'Dry foods suits every man, and I am a man, and such-and-such food is dry' as a composite universal premiss. If we do this, we are drawn up short by 'I am

[8] Against Grant and Joachim, I take it that διαφέρει τὸ καθόλου doesn't mean: there are two kinds of universal premisses (this would need feminine), but rather: two different universal *terms*. So Ross: 'There are two kinds of universal term: one is predicable of the agent, the other of the object.'

a man' which is indubitably particular, being singular. Of course αὐτὸς ἄνθρωπος is only Rassow's conjecture, and it may well be possible to emend the text into something suitably universal. But it is much simpler if we take the universal as being simply 'Dry food suits every man', and the rest as a composite particular premiss.

This fits well the patterns of the practical syllogism in the *De Anima* (434a16). There we are told that a practical syllogism contains a universal judgement which says

such-and-such a one should do so-and-so

and an individual (καθ' ἕκαστα) which says

this now is so-and-so, and I am such-and-such.

'Dry food suits every man' seems recognizable as an instance of the universal pattern (if we imagine 'should eat' for συμφέρει) and αὐτὸς ἄνθρωπος is a particular instance of κἀγὼ δὲ τοιόσδε.[9] But the other part of the particular premiss which appears atomic in the *De Anima* is divided in the *Ethics* passage. 'This now is so-and-so' appears as 'such-and-such food is dry, and this now is such-and-such'.

I suggest, then, that the passage 1146b35-1147a7 is merely an expansion of the first passage 1146b30-37, as the parallel between their conclusions suggests. First, we are told that you can have knowledge in general without applying it to the particular case. Then we are told in detail how this happens. Action, always particular, is based on two premisses of a practical syllogism, one a universal principle and the other a composite particular premiss. The universal principle is applied (less universal instances are recognized as falling under it: e.g. chicken suits every man; and perhaps also: chicken suits me); but the particular premiss, or one of its components (e.g. chicken is dry food), though possessed, is not applied. That is to say, the piece of singular knowledge—that *this* is chicken—is missing.[10]

Cook Wilson and others have argued that these passages cannot be by Aristotle because inconsistent with his general picture of incontinence as a conflict between reason and desire. Here there

---

[9] Not one which it would take much trouble to ascertain (cf. *De Mot An.* 701a26). A more interesting instance would be Aquinas' *oportet filium honorare parentes*. (*Comm. Eth. ad loc.*).

[10] ἢ οὐκ ἔχει ἢ οὐκ ἐνεργεῖ.. Applied to knowledge of the individual, the distinction must be between failing to recognize this food (at all) as chicken, and failure to recognize it when in front of me on a particular occasion.

THE PRACTICAL SYLLOGISM AND INCONTINENCE 39

is no conflict since the judgement of reason is not actual. Moreover, according to Book III, someone who is ignorant of the particular circumstances of his action acts unwillingly and is to be pitied; whereas the incontinent man acts willingly and is to be blamed.

Two possible answers may be made to this. The first is to point out that according to the doctrine of Book III ignorance is not always excusable, but only ignorance for which the agent is not to blame (1113b24). However, the ignorance which Aristotle considers blameworthy always appears to be ignorance concerning the *major* premiss: ignorance of what one should do, or ignorance of what is in the laws (1110b27–1111a1; 1113b34). Ignorance of the minor premiss is held to excuse[11] and so if incontinence consisted in ignorance of the minor premiss it would be excusable.

It seems preferable, therefore, to admit that as a solution of the problem of incontinence the passage 1146b31–47a4 is inconsistent with Aristotle's teaching in other books of the *Nicomachean Ethics*. But in fact there is no reason to believe that these paragraphs are put forward as a solution to that problem: the incontinent man is not mentioned in them. Aristotle is simply explaining *one* sense in which a man can εἰδὼς ἃ μὴ δεῖ πράττειν. It is only with the ἔτι of line 10 that he comes to the case in point: and from that line he goes on to present two different solutions, most probably to cater for two different cases.[12]

Aristotle's own explanation of ἀκρασία—on this view—is given in the two passages 1147a10 to 1147a24, and 1147a24 to 1147b5. He begins by drawing a distinction between two kinds of ἕξις within the class of ἕξεις which he has already distinguished from ἐνέργειαι. Besides the possessing-but-not-exercising mentioned above, there is another sort of possessing-and-not-exercising,

---

[11] Unless we take ὁμοίως δὲ καὶ ἐν τοῖς ἄλλοις in 1114a1 to refer to culpable inadvertence to the particular. But the context suggests that the ἄλλα are non-legal moral principles which the agent forgets because of being careless about observing them. In 1111a10 ff. cases which *we* would regard as culpable inadvertence are put forward as cases which deserve ἔλεος.

[12] Oresme gives an example to illustrate this passage which shows that he takes Aristotle to be referring to culpable inadvertence here: *Si comme un marinier peut savoir ceste universale: Tout peril est a eviter. Et avecques ce, ceste singuliere: il a peril en tel lieu. Et peut bien considerer a l'universale quand il vient en lieu perilleux; mais par inadvertance, il ne considere pas quand il est en tel lieu, ou ceste singuliere: tel lieu est perilleux.* (Commentary on Ethics, ed. Albert D. Mennes, 371 ff.).

D

the state of those asleep or mad or drunk.[13] Those who have learnt geometry and are sober, awake, and in their right mind have the ἕξις of geometry even when they are not actually doing geometry. This ἕξις enables them to do geometry whenever they want, provided they are not prevented by external circumstances (*De An.* 417a26 ff.). But people who have learnt geometry and are now drunk, asleep, or insane are in a different position. They are not in the same position as those who have never learnt geometry at all, and so in one sense they have the ἕξις of geometry. But they cannot exercise this ἕξις when they want; nor are they prevented by something external to themselves. They are prevented by an internal state for whose cessation they must wait before being able once again to exercise their ἕξις (Cf. *De Gen. An.* 736a9–11). The distinction here made by Aristotle became a scholastic commonplace as the distinction between *habitus solutus* and *habitus ligatus*.[14]

Aristotle's first solution of the problem of ἀκρασία is to suggest that in the incontinent the ἕξις of the moral principles is a *habitus ligatus* like the ἕξις of geometry in a sleeping geometrician. Like sleep and drunkenness, anger and sexual desire alter our bodily condition; sometimes such passions cause fits of madness. An objection might be made to this that incontinent men, while acting incontinently, sometimes proclaim the moral principles they are violating. If they thus display the ἐνέργεια of moral knowledge, must they not *a fortiori* have the corresponding ἕξις in its unfettered state? Aristotle replies that the utterance of the appropriate sentences is no guarantee that the ἐπιστήμη is fully possessed. Drunkards and madmen recite geometrical proofs and poems of Empedocles; learners whose state of mind does not yet deserve to be called knowledge repeat what they are told; actors on the stage recite speeches they do not really endorse. So, the incontinent may utter the correct sentiments without his ἐπιστήμη being more than a *habitus ligatus*.

[13] Cook Wilson thought that this passage was merely a doublet of 1146b31 ff., making the same distinction ἕξις / ἐνέργεια. But Cook Wilson's view is refuted by 1147a12, where Aristotle says that within possessing-and-not-exercising we see a different sort of possessing, as it were possessing and not possessing (ὥστε καὶ ἔχειν πως καὶ μὴ ἔχειν).
[14] The distinction between the non-use of the former and the latter is well brought out by the Aldine Scholiast ἐκεῖ μὲν εἶχε τὴν ἐπιστήμην, ἑκὼν δὲ οὐκ ἐνήργει. ἐνταῦθα δὲ ἔχει μὲν τὴν ἐπιστήμην, ἄκων δὲ οὐκ ἐνεργεῖ. (*Comm. in Ar. Graeca* XX, 419).

THE PRACTICAL SYLLOGISM AND INCONTINENCE 41

In the paraphrase I have just given, I have taken it that οἱ λόγοι οἱ ἀπὸ τῆς ἐπιστήμης uttered by the incontinent are the universal premisses of practical syllogisms, and not the fragmentary minors illustrated at 1147a7. It is surely more likely that Aristotle is suggesting that the incontinent babbles unmeaningly 'mustn't commit adultery' rather than 'this is someone else's wife'.[15]

This solution explains why it is no use simply to *talk* to the incontinent. You can't talk people out of madness or drunkeness either. But there are two difficulties. The first is that the solution seems to be inconsistent with what Aristotle says elsewhere; the second, that it seems inadequate to the φαινόμενα. If the universal premiss is obscured by something other than the evil desire, then there is no conflict between reason and passion as described in 1102b14–25. If, on the other hand, it is obscured by the desire itself, then it is hard to see how Aristotle could go on in 1147b16 to say that the κυρίως ἐπιστήμη was not dragged about by passion and so Socrates was right after all.

Moreover, if incontinence is like madness, it is hard to see how it is voluntary and blameworthy. If it is like drunkenness, to be sure, then it can be blamed: a drunk can be punished because it was in his power not to get drunk (1113b32); so perhaps an incontinent man can be punished because a truly virtuous man would not have evil desires. On the other hand, a continent man has evil desires; and again, it is odd that Aristotle should have compared incontinence indifferently to drunkenness and madness, when the two are different in the crucial matter of voluntariness.

Some cases of people doing what they say is wrong are no doubt cases where they are acting under the influence of a bodily disturbance to madness near allied.[16] But this is hardly the normal case of incontinence: indeed it does not seem to be a genuine

---

[15] So the paraphrast and Albert (*'meretrix honestam dicit esse continentiam'*); against, Aquinas and Burleigh, who speak of *'habitus in singularibus ligatus'*. Joachim sits on the fence: the incontinent utters 'the words of practical wisdom'.

[16] It would be helpful to know whether the bodily conditions spoken of in 1147a16 were meant to be normal or pathological. The Aldine Scholiast speaks of the red eyes of rage and the pale face of the lover (*Comm. in Ar. Graeca* XX, 420); Albert says '*in concupiscentia venereorum constitutus, totum spiritum animalem protendit in venerea, ita quod etiam conceptu talium formarum totum corpus immutatur: quod maxime sentitur in genitalibus, et forma in tali spiritu accepta fortiter ligat ad venerea.*'

case of incontinence at all. To such people the appropriate reaction would appear to be not punishment but treatment: as we might say, δεῖ παρὰ τῶν φυσιολόγων ἀκούειν. (1147b9). But this makes 1147a10-25 quite inadequate as a solution to the philosophical problem.[17]

It is hard to know whether Aristotle ever put it forward as such. If he did, he had second thoughts about it which are incorporated in the quite different solution of lines 25 ff. But it is possible that lines 10-25 are meant merely as an account of one type of case which might be thought to fall under the rubric of ἀκρασία: the case of pathological inability to conform to one's moral professions. In that case, the problem of incontinence proper is not attacked until line 25. This interpretation would accord well with Aristotle's insistence in Book III that action out of desire is not necessarily a case of psychological compulsion (1110b9, 1111a24).[18]

Allan, in 'The Practical Syllogism', paraphrases the passage thus:

'Further, the cause (of ἀκρασία) may be viewed in this way. One judgement is universal, the other bears upon particulars which belong to the sphere of perception. When these judgements coalesce into one, it is necessary that, just as elsewhere [sc. in the sphere of theory] the mind assents to a conclusion, so here, when the premisses are practical, it should at once act. E.g. if 'one ought to taste everything sweet' and 'here is a particular sweet thing', it is necessary that one who has the power and is not [sc. physically] hindered should at once proceed to act.' (*Autour d'Aristote*, 327).

With two exceptions, this translation seems to me excellent. But both *scilicets* appear mistaken. There seems no ground for translating ἔνθα as 'elsewhere' and glossing it as [sc. in the sphere of theory]. The reference to theory is quite irrelevant to the con-

---

[17] The main difference between madness/drunkenness/sleep and ἀκρασία is that the former states result in an obfuscation of knowledge in general, or over a wide area; ἀκρασία in at most the obfuscation of knowledge of a particular principle.

[18] If 1147a10-24 deals with pathological, and 1147a24-b5 with normal incontinence, may not to view incontinence φυσικῶς (line 24) be to look at its natural cause—ἐπιθυμία—as opposed to its παρὰ φύσιν causes—the ἀλλοιώσεις βίαιοι of the near-insane?

text; moreover, Allan himself has to say 'the expression in this passage is somewhat loose, since it might suggest that in demonstration, as well as in action, there are minor premises which have a particular, perceptible subject; and this, we know, is not Aristotle's doctrine' (328).

But if 'ἔνθα' does not mean 'in theoretical cases', what does it mean, and what does ἐν δὲ ταῖς ποιητικαῖς (line 28) contrast with? The contrast with theory, I have said, is irrelevant: what *is* relevant is a contrast between practical syllogisms with positive and negative conclusions—i.e. with conclusions of the form 'Do such-and-such' and of the form 'Don't do such-and-such'. In line 29 Aristotle gives an example of a positive one, and in line 31 ff. of a negative one. It is only, of course, in the case of a positive conclusion that a practical syllogism, if operative, must lead to action—except in the sense in which refraining from action is itself an action. We know from the first two examples in the *De Motu Animalium* (701a13–15) that Aristotle was conscious of the distinction between the two sorts of practical syllogism: the second of those examples runs: 'no man should walk now, I am a man', so he stays put.[19] The sense of the present passage, then, is that when the two judgements coalesce, in all cases the soul must assert[20] the conclusion, and if the conclusion is positive, the man acts at once. ἔνθα has its common sense of *thereupon* —at once, whatever case is in question; the μὲν and the δὲ marks the contrast between the general case and a specific instance. What is ποιητικαί contrasted with? Not, I suggest, either θεωρητικαί or πρακτικαί but κωλυτικαί. Four lines further on Aristotle uses κωλύουσα to describe a negative universal premiss; and though I cannot find an instance of the word κωλυτικός itself in precisely this sense, the contrast between ποιητικός and κωλυτικός in general is frequent in Aristotle (Cf. 1096b12, *Rhet.* 1362a24).

The use of κωλύουσα in line 32 also suggests that Allan's second *scilicet* is mistaken. κωλυόμενον in line 31 probably does not mean 'physically hindered' but 'prevented by a conflicting internal factor'. Otherwise, the verb is used to refer to quite

---

[19] Possibly, however, Aristotle has in mind a man *ceasing* to walk—this would explain also why he calls ἠρεμία a πρᾶξις in line 16.

[20] What sort of necessity is the ἀνάγκη? Is it what we would call logical necessity? Burleigh: *Ex opinione universali in actu et opinione singulari in actu necessario sequitur opus, non sicut conclusio ex praemissis, sed tamen sicut posterius sequitur ad prius, ut pluvia sequitur ad nubem.*

different factors in line 31 and line 32; and in line 31 μὴ κωλυόμενον becomes merely a repetition of δυνάμενον.

'Must taste everything sweet'—it has been observed—sounds absurd unless restricted to a particular situation (Anscombe, *Intention*, p. 65). But pretty clearly this is only an abbreviation of a universal premiss,[21] which set out fully on the lines of the *De Anima* and 1147a5 would be of the form παντὸς γλυκέος γεύεσθαι δεῖ τὸν τοιοῦτον where the restriction to the particular situation would be made clear in the substitution for the variable τοιοῦτος. Similarly, τουτὶ δὲ γλυκὺ ὡς ἕν τι τῶν καθ' ἕκαστον suggests that τουτὶ δὲ γλυκύ is only *one* of the atomic propositions which go to make up the composite minor. (Before actually tasting something, you could not *perceive* it was sweet except by perceiving it was such-and-such, e.g. sugar, and knowing that sugar was sweet.)

In the passage which follows (ὅταν οὖν ἡ μὲν καθόλου . . . 1147a 31) it is often assumed that there are two syllogisms in question, one of which has as its universal premiss 'everything sweet is pleasant', and another with a different universal premiss (perhaps 'nothing sweet should be tasted') which is described by Aristotle as 'the universal forbidding us to taste'. Thus, for instance, Gauthier and Jolif (p. 613). The clearest statement of this view known to me is that of the paraphrast. 'When the universal premiss forbids to taste—the one which says, nothing sweet should be tasted—the other, i.e. the universal premiss says: everything sweet is pleasant'. (*Comm. in Ar. Graeca*, XIX, 141). The belief that two syllogisms are in question seems common to almost all commentators,[22] and some translators make Aristotle say so more or less explicitly. Thus, Thomson's Penguin translation reads 'Now there may be simultaneously present in the mind two universal judgements, one saying "You must not taste", the other "Every sweet thing is pleasant"'. Ross, in his translation is more cautious. 'When, then, the universal opinion is present in us forbidding us to taste, and there is also the opinion that "everything sweet is pleasant" . . .' But in his book *Aristotle* he

[21] Not, as Burnet says, 'the major premiss of ἀκολασία'.
[22] The only disagreement seems to have been whether the second syllogism could rightly be called the syllogism of desire or not. Burleigh denies this: *videtur quod concupiscentia cum sit passio existens in parte sensitiva non habet aliquam universalem in quam inclinetur sed solum inclinetur a particulari. Ipse tamen incontinens habet duas propositiones universales et sub una sumit minorem in practice syllogizando.*

paraphrases: 'You may have a major which says "nothing that is x should be tasted" but the minor "this is x" you may not know at all, or know only in the remote sense in which, as we have seen, a drunken man may be said to know "the verses of Empedocles"; and on the other hand you may have another major premiss "everything that is sweet is pleasant" and a minor "this is sweet", and you may have a desire for what is pleasant".' (p. 223). Walsh, in *Aristotle's Conception of Moral Weakness*, 106, complains that the text is obscure. 'It gives the syllogism which issues in the action of the morally weak man clearly enough. The universal premiss is 'all sweet things are pleasant' and the particular premiss is "that is sweet". But it does not give the opposing syllogism explicitly'. And he has whole sections devoted to 'What is the suppressed premiss?' and 'How are the two universal premisses opposed?' (106–9, 109–11). Similarly, Aquinas in his commentary *ad loc*: '*Sit ergo ita, quod ex parte rationis proponatur una universalis prohibens gustare dulce inordinate, puta si dicatur, nullum dulce est gustandum extra horam. Sed ex parte concupiscentiae ponatur quod omne dulce est delectabile, quod est per se quaesitum a concupiscentia.*'

The text does not seem to me to justify the assumption that there are two syllogisms in question. It appears unnatural to read ἡ μὲν καθόλου as meaning 'the universal of one syllogism' as opposed to the universal of another; it would most naturally be read as 'the universal premiss' as opposed to the particular premiss (cf. 1147a25 and *De An.* 434a16). What has prevented people from taking it in the natural way is the occurrence of πᾶν ('*everything* sweet is pleasant') and the belief that practical syllogisms should have just two simple premisses. But as we have seen, the syllogism of 1147a5 has an explicitly composite minor; and the syllogism of 1147a28 gives the appearance of being an abbreviation of one with a composite minor. Moreover, in the composite minor of 1147a5, though the word πᾶν does not occur, the proposition 'such and such food is dry' must in fact be (what we would call) universal if the argument is to lead to any conclusion. Again, in E.N. 6 we are told that φρόνησις concerns not only the particular but the individual (τὰ καθ' ἕκαστα). As an example of knowledge of the universal we are given the knowledge that light meats are digestible and wholesome; as an example of knowledge of the individual we are given the knowledge of what meats (e.g. chicken) are light.[23] But the knowledge that chicken is light is—to our way of expression—as universal a piece of knowledge as the knowledge that everything sweet is pleasant.[24]

It seems possible, therefore, that in this passage we have here not two conflicting syllogisms, but a single syllogism which has two premisses: the universal premiss which forbids tasting, and a composite minor premiss which says 'everything sweet is pleasant and this is sweet'.[25] This interpretation seems to me made almost certain by a later passage, 1149a32 ff., where Aristotle is arguing that incontinence of anger is more rational than simple incontinence. 'For argument or imagination informs us that we have been insulted or slighted, and anger, reasoning as it were that something like this must be fought against, boils up straightway; while appetite, if argument or perception merely says that an object is pleasant, springs to the enjoyment of it. Therefore anger obeys argument in a sense, but appetite does not.'[26] The passage in Ch. III concerns simple incontinence; the passage in Ch. VI tells us that in simple incontinence desire does not reason. Therefore, there is no syllogism of desire in Ch. III, but only the one syllogism of reason. Otherwise, desire no less than anger would be ὥσπερ συλλογισάμενος and Aristotle's contrast would fall to the ground. Moreover, if πᾶν γλυκὺ ἡδύ were a practical universal parallel to the prohibiting universal, then the incontinent, acting incontinently on this, would be acting προαιρούμενος which is what we are told he does not.[27]

If only one syllogism is in question, what is 'the universal premiss forbidding to taste'? As Walsh says, it can hardly be

[23] 1141b20. Trendelenburg's deletion of κοῦφα καὶ clearly rests on a misunderstanding of the text.

[24] Aristotle's teaching in the Prior Analytics is that indefinite premisses are to be treated as particular (26a29, 29a27). (Cf. Luckasiewicz, *Aristotle's Syllogistic*, 5). But this passage makes nonsense unless τὰ ὀρνίθεια κοῦφα means '*every*thing ὀρνίθειον is light. Perhaps the presence of the article, like the presence of πᾶν, turns a proposition from indefinite into universal, for purposes of deduction.

[25] This was first suggested to me by Mr. Alan Simcock.

[26] The relevance of this passage was pointed out to me by Mr. Colin Macleod.

[27] 1111b14 etc. Of course the incontinent does make some προαιρέσεις, e.g. wanting to seduce a woman, he may after deliberation choose means to this end (cf. 1142b20). But if you ask him then why he wants to seduce the woman, he doesn't answer this by communicating *further* deliberation; in this he differs from the intemperate, who will say: to seduce this woman is pleasant, and one should pursue pleasure. The incontinent acts for pleasure, but doesn't give pleasure as his reason for acting—so the pursuit of pleasure is not the result of a προαίρεσις.

'don't taste *this*'. Various suggestions have been put forward. The paraphrast proposed: taste nothing sweet. Aquinas suggested 'Taste nothing sweet between meals'—obviously he was anxious to find a principle which a man might plausibly adopt. Ross, more cautiously, 'nothing that is x should be tasted'. But if we are right in taking 'everything sweet is pleasant, and this is sweet' as the particular premiss, then the universal premiss must be something like 'taste nothing pleasant'.

This may seem an excessively puritanical premiss to have occurred to Aristotle.[28] But the premiss which he attributes to the intemperate man is 'pursue the present pleasure'. The premiss of the incontinent man is presumably the contradictory of the premiss of the intemperate man: the contradictory of 'pursue the present pleasure' appears to be 'do not pursue the present pleasure'. Unfortunately, this latter imperative is ambiguous: it may mean 'Do not pursue every pleasure that presents itself'—and in this case it really is the contradictory of the intemperate premiss; or it may mean 'whatever pleasure presents itself, do not pursue it'; in which case it involves, as a particular instance, 'taste nothing pleasant'. We have already discussed the multiple ambiguity in this area; given the pitfalls, it is possible that Aristotle did not distinguish between these two different imperatives. If this seems too great an error to attribute to him, we can remind ourselves that in any case 'mustn't taste anything pleasant' would be only an abbreviation, on *De Anima* principles, for a universal premiss which would contain some reference to a man of a certain kind or in a certain situation.

The minor premiss, on the view I am defending, is 'everything sweet is pleasant, and this is sweet': this corresponds to 'such-and-such food is dry, and this is such-and-such' in 47a4.[29] From this minor premiss it at once follows that this is pleasant. Two things result from this: first, that this falls under the prohibition of the universal premiss; secondly, that it is an object of ἐπιθυμία which is by definition ἡδέος ὄρεξις. This minor premiss —unlike the minor premiss of 47a7—comes into operation

[28] But if pleasant means 'bodily pleasant'—as in the context it obviously does—then one can find such puritanical statements in the Aristotelian tradition—αἱ δ'ἡδοναὶ αἱ σωματικαὶ ψεκταί (M. M. 1202b8).

[29] What we want, in the case of the incontinent, is a minor premiss which, taken in conjunction with the intemperate major—which he has not got—would lead to action. And this is precisely what 'Everything sweet is pleasant and this is sweet' would do.

(αὕτη δὲ ἐνεργεῖ, line 33). That is to say—if our earlier interpretation of the sense of ἐνεργεῖ is correct—it is applied to the particular case. And so, we are told in the text, it does: the conclusion from universal and particular premisses is drawn: ἡ μὲν οὖν λέγει φεύγειν τοῦτο.[30] ἡ μὲν must be either the conclusion arising from the two combined premisses, as in 47a27; or perhaps the *psyche*, which we are told necessarily asserts the conclusion once the two premisses come together (1147a27). The conclusion is particular and practical: it is φεύγειν τοῦτο.[31] φεύγειν is a technical term of Aristotle's for the expression of a decision negativing action (1139a22 f.). But though the conclusion forbidding action is drawn, it does not find effect in action; for the man is overcome by desire; he can be set in motion either by reasoning or by irrational desire.[32] Thus in this case we do, after all, have a full-blooded conflict between reason and desire: the syllogism of reason runs through to its conclusion; but the conclusion is not carried out in action because of the opposition of unreasoning desire. If it be objected to this interpretation that according to the *De Motu Animalium* the conclusion of a practical syllogism *is* an action (701a13), we can reply that according to the same paragraph of the same book the words ἱμάτιον ποιητέον are the conclusion of a practical syllogism (701a20); so that when Aristotle says that the conclusion of a practical syllogism is an action, he need only mean that the conclusion of a practical syllogism must be the description of an action to be done.

No conclusion is drawn *in favour* of action: the incontinent just acts.[33] Yet the action of the incontinent, as here described, is partly the result of his reasoning. For without the minor premiss—that this is sweet, and what is sweet is pleasant—there would not be the awareness that this is pleasant nor the subsequent desire. Desire arises, as it were, because it hears the reason say that this is pleasant (1149a35). Thus Aristotle can say that ἀκρασία is in a way the result of λόγος and δόξα: it is the result of

---

[30] Indeed, if the conclusion were *not* drawn, how could it be said that the incontinent man's προαίρεσις was virtuous (1152a17)? Merely to have a correct universal is not to make a προαίρεσις unless a conclusion is drawn.
[31] The conclusion of a προαίρεσις can be a particular action—such as destroying Troy, if only Troy weren't already destroyed (1139b7).
[32] It is thus I interpret 1147a35, following Ramsauer, against Stewart.
[33] See the long and extremely subtle discussion of Buridan (*Questiones super X libros ethicorum*) in the appendix ('*nunc ergo regredior*') to the 7th question on the 7th book.

THE PRACTICAL SYLLOGISM AND INCONTINENCE 49

the (virtuous) practical syllogism and in particular of its minor premiss the particular δόξα. The particular premiss, though it gives rise to the ἐπιθυμία which fights against reason, is not itself *per se* opposed to the temperate universal premiss; it is only the desire, not the opinion which provokes it, which fights against the right reasoning embodied in the practical syllogism (1147b1–3).[34]

The passage which follows (1147b5–9) seems to me clearly out of place.[35] 'The explanation of how the ignorance is dissolved and the incontinent man regains his knowledge, is the same as in the case of the man drunk or asleep and is not peculiar to this condition; we must go to the students of natural science for it.' This relates to the explanation of ἀκρασία in 47a10–24, not to the one just given. If the later explanation represents Aristotle's second thoughts, it seems that it has been placed by his editor not quite in the right place: the sentence just quoted should precede it and not follow it. The next sentence (ἐπεὶ δ' ἡ τελευταία πρότασις, 1147b9 ff.) comes well after both accounts, provided only that we take τελευταία πρότασις to mean not the last premiss, but the conclusion.[36] The conclusion is indeed δόξα αἰσθητοῦ (it concerns the object of perception τοῦτο) and κυρία πράξεων (it contains the practical imperative φεύγειν). There are two cases of ἀκρασία: one—described in 47a10–24—where the conclusion is not drawn (οὐκ ἔχει); the other where it is drawn verbally but has no more effect on action than the babblings of a drunkard (οὕτως ἔχει ὡς οὐκ ἦν τὸ ἔχειν ἐπίστασθαι).

Yet both Aristotle's general doctrine of conflict and Socrates' doctrine of knowledge emerge unscathed. There is a genuine conflict, because ἐπιθυμία fights against a conclusion reached by

---

[34] Punctuate ... ἀλλὰ κατὰ συμβεβηκός. ἡ γὰρ ἐπιθυμία ἐναντία, ἀλλ' οὐχ ἡ δόξα, τῷ ὀρθῷ λόγῳ.

[35] So too Gauthier and Jolif and others. The reference to ἄγνοια suggests misplacement.

[36] τελευταία πρότασις would more naturally mean the last (minor) *premiss*; but it cannot mean that here, since we are told that the minor 'this is sweet' is not only present but active (1145a32) and there is no suggestion in the text that there is any other minor ἐπὶ τοῦ πράγματος apart from 'all sweet things are pleasant'. (So Burleigh: *propositio circa quam decipitur incontinens et cuius ignorantiam habet non est minor sillogismi practici sed est conclusio . . . circa minorem huius sillogismi non decipitur incontinens, quia bene novit quod hoc est dulce, sed circa conclusionem decipitur.* So too, in effect, the paraphrast—contradicting himself—when he says that what the incontinent babbles like a drunkard is ἡ μοιχεία αὕτη κακόν ἐστιν). πρότασις frequently means 'proposition'; cf. for instance, Topics 105a20. At 105b22 even the question πότερον δεῖ τοῖς γονεῦσιν μᾶλλον ἢ τοῖς νόμοις πειθαρχεῖν ἐὰν διαφωνῶσιν is called a πρότασις ἠθική.

reasoning. Yet knowledge is not dragged about like a slave, because the conclusion which ἐπιθυμία overcomes is neither general (since it concerns *this*) nor epistemonic (since it contains the practical imperative). On the common interpretations, line 15 has been a crux. It is often translated 'it is not in the presence of what is thought to be knowledge proper that the affection of incontinence arises, nor is it this that is "dragged about" as a result of the state of passion'. For these who believe that Aristotle's explanation of ἀκρασία appeals to ignorance of the particular premiss, this comes very oddly: for in such a case the universal knowledge *is* present (1147a2, a32). Stewart, accordingly, proposed to emend γίνεται into περιγίνεται: but that makes the first clause say exactly the same as the second. On my view, the meaning is 'It is not as a result of the presence of what seems really to be knowledge[37] that the passion arises'—i.e. it is not the mental utterance of the major, but of the minor premiss, which gives rise to the ἐπιθυμία. The major premiss is not dragged about by passion[38]—it *does* operate, i.e. is applied to the less general case (cf. above p. 170).

If all this is correct, it is wrong either to blame or to praise Aristotle for failing to consider the case of a man acting in a way which he fully knows at the time to be wrong. For he considers just such a case when he discusses the case in which the conclusion of the practical syllogism is drawn. Walsh concludes his book on moral weakness in Aristotle by saying that the absence of the concept of the will produces a serious limitation in his analysis of ἀκρασία. But if my interpretation is correct, the alleged limitations of Aristotle's account are often limitations of his commentators.

[37] i.e. that which, in the view which Aristotle shares with Socrates, is alone really to be called ἐπιστήμη viz. the universal.
[38] Nor, on my view, is the minor premiss dragged about by passion (since it, too, leads on to the conclusion). But Aristotle does not say that it is: he wrote not ἡ αἰσθητική but τῆς αἰσθητικῆς.

ARISTOTLE ON HAPPINESS

'From the dawn of philosophy,' wrote Mill, 'the question concerning the *summum bonum*, or, what is the same thing, concerning the foundation of morality, has been accounted the main problem in speculative thought and has occupied the most gifted intellects.' For some time the most gifted intellects have been averse to putting questions concerning the foundation of morality in terms of the *summum bonum*. But recently there has been some sign of a return of interest in the notion of a supreme good or happiness. We might instance the chapter on 'The Good of Man' in von Wright's *Varieties of Goodness*, (1963), B. A. O. Williams, 'Aristotle on the Good' (*Ph. Q.*, Oct. 1962), W. F. R. Hardie, 'The Final Good in Aristotle's Ethics' (*Philos.*, October 1965).

The notion of a supreme good is, I shall later argue, only one of the elements which have contributed to the formation of our concept of happiness. None the less, I shall follow the authors I have mentioned in approaching the topic via Aristotle's discussion.

Aristotle defined the supreme good (*tagathon kai to ariston*) as 'an end of action which is desired for its own sake, while everything else is desired for the sake of it' (*E.N.* 1094a19). *Prima facie*, one can interpret the contention that there is a supreme good in three ways. One may take it as a logical truth, as an empirical observation, or as a moral imperative. Someone who says that there is a supreme good, in Aristotle's sense, may mean that as a matter of logical truth there is a single end which is aimed at in every choice of a human being. He may mean, on the other hand, that every man does as a matter of contingent fact have a single aim in every one of his choices. Or, finally, he may mean that every man should, under pain of being unreasonable or immoral, aim at a single end in each of his choices. Writers on the *summum bonum* do not always make clear which of these alternatives they have in mind.

Moreover, each of these alternatives is itself ambiguous. Is the 'single end' in question an end which is, or ought to be, common to every choice of every man? Or is it merely an end which governs every choice of each particular man, but which perhaps differs from man to man? The first of the foregoing alternatives, for instance, may be taken in two ways. It may be a strong thesis to the effect that it is a logical truth that every man, in every choice, aims at a single end which is common to all choices of all men. Or it may be the weaker thesis that each man, in each of his choices, pursues a single end, but one which is perhaps proper to himself.

Aristotle is sometimes thought to have presented the doctrine of the supreme good in a form which is equivalent to the stronger of the two logical theses just distinguished. It does seem to be a necessary truth that one cannot choose everything for the sake of something else: chains of reasoning about means and ends must come to a halt somewhere. Aristotle alludes to this truth on the first page of the *Nicomachean Ethics* (1094a18).

'If, then, there is some end of the things we do, which we desire for its own sake (everything else being desired for the sake of this), and if we do not choose everything for the sake of something else (for at that rate the process would go on to infinity, so that our desire would be empty and vain), clearly this must be the good and the chief good.' (tr. Ross).

This passage has been taken to contain a (fallacious) proof of the existence of a single supreme end of action. Thus Geach writes, 'It is clear that Aristotle thinks himself entitled to pass from "Every series whose successive terms stand in the relation *chosen for the sake of* has a last term" to "There is something that is the last term of every series whose successive terms stand in the relation *chosen for the sake of*"' (*Journal of the Philosophical Association*, V, 112 1958). Such a transition is clearly fallacious. Every road leads somewhere: it does not follow that there is somewhere—e.g., Rome—to which all roads lead.

To convict Aristotle of this fallacy one must assume that he is offering the second if-clause 'we do not choose everything for the sake of something else' as a reason for the hypothesis in the first if-clause 'there is some end of the things we do which we desire for its own sake'. But this, Williams, argues, it is not necessary to do: the second hypothesis may be a consequence of, not a reason for, the first. Von Wright and Hardie agree with Williams in acquitting Aristotle of the fallacy attributed to him by Geach. Von Wright points out that if Aristotle here accepts the conclusion that there is one and only one end of all chains of practical reasoning, then he contradicts himself. Clearly, happiness, for Aristotle, is at least *one* supreme end. But 'Aristotle also admits that there are ends, other than happiness, which we pursue for their own sake. He mentions pleasure and honour among them' (*The Varieties of Goodness*, 89, citing *E.N.*, 1097b1–2). Aristotle seems, then, guiltless of the fallacy attributed to him, though it entrapped some of his followers, notably Aquinas (*S.T.*, Ia IIae, I, 4–6).

It seems, in fact, to be false that it is logically necessary that there should be some one end which a man pursues in each of his choices. It might be thought that if we made our end vague and general enough, we might avoid this conclusion. To act voluntarily is to act because one wants to, either because one wants the action for its own sake, or because one wants something to be gained by the action. Therefore, it might be argued, there is some one end which we pursue whenever we act voluntarily, namely the satisfaction of our wants. But this argument is fallacious. If all that is being said is that when I act out of desire for x, then I am pursuing the satisfaction of my desire for x, it has not been established that I am pursuing a single end in all my actions; for there are as many different satisfactions as there are desires to satisfy. If, on the other hand, it is alleged that whenever a man acts he must be pursuing a goal which consists in the satisfaction of *all* his desires, then the theory, so far from being necessarily true, is not even empirically true. For it is perfectly possible not to have as a goal the satisfaction of all one's desires, and indeed positively to hope that not all one's desires will be satisfied. Russell, for instance, in *The Conquest of Happiness*, says 'to be without some of the things you want is an indispensable part of happiness'. In so far as Russell wants to be happy, he must, in conformity with his dictum, want to be without some of the things he wants.

There may seem to be a certain inconsistency here. It is akin to what logicians call ω-inconsistency—the sort of inconsistency which is illustrated by the sentence 'he was wearing a glove on one hand, and he was not wearing a glove on his left hand, and he was not wearing a glove on his right hand'.[1] In persons, if not in systems, ω-inconsistency seems to me no bad thing. Modesty seems to demand that we should hold ω-inconsistent beliefs: *e.g.*, that we should believe that some of our beliefs are false. Only a man who knows himself infallible could have reasonable confidence that all his beliefs were true. Similarly, patience seems to demand that we should have ω-inconsistent desires: at least, that we should be willing that some of our desires should be dissatisfied. But whether or not such ω-inconsistency in desires is desirable, it is certainly possible. If so, it cannot be a logical truth that in everything we do we seek a single aim of total satisfaction.

Williams has argued that Aristotle accepted the thesis that whatever is pursued for a single aim, not on the basis of the fallacious argument about chains of practical reasoning, but on the basis of the considerations about function in 1097b25 ff. This account of Aristotle's argument seems to me mistaken. It is tendentious to translate '*ergon*' as *function*; we need not credit Aristotle with believing that men serve a purpose. If we translate '*ergon*' as *characteristic activity*, then the burden of the passage is as follows. Where an F has a characteristic activity, φ-ing, then a good F is an F which φs well. Different classes of men, and different parts of a man, each have their characteristic activity. Presumably, then, man has a characteristic activity: this must be an activity of the rational soul, else it would be common to animals and plants and so not characteristic of man as such. The characteristic activity of the good man, therefore, will be the good activity of the rational soul. Therefore, the good for man (*to anthropinon agathon*) will be the activity of the soul in accordance with excellence.

The surprising step in this argument is the identification of the good for man with the characteristic activity of the good man. Surely, we feel inclined to object, what is good for sculptors (e.g., adequate remuneration and good living conditions) is quite different from what the good sculptor does (e.g. sculpt well). But presumably Aristotle would reply that this merely showed the

---

[1] Since the number of hands is finite this sentence is not itself ω-inconsistent.

difference between what was good for sculptors *qua* men and what was good for them *qua* sculptors. What it is good for a man, *qua* man, to do is what the good man in fact does *qua* good man. But what the good man does is what all men *should* do: nothing follows about what all men *do*. The argument from the *ergon* of man, then, cannot show that, as a matter of fact or logic, all men pursue whatever they pursue for the sake of happiness.

Even as a matter of fact, Aristotle did not believe that men seek a single end in all their actions.[2] The incontinent man who is described in Book Seven, pursues pleasure in some of his actions, though the end he sets for his life is other than pleasure. However, we are told that the incontinent man does not *choose* to seek pleasure, so perhaps, it might be argued, Aristotle would support the weaker thesis that whatever is *chosen* is chosen for the sake of happiness. But even this thesis is ruled out by the passage at 1097a34 which Williams himself quotes. There we are told that while happiness is always chosen for its own sake and never for the sake of anything else, honour and pleasure and reason and virtue are chosen both for their own sake and for the sake of happiness. This seems to refute Williams' claim that Aristotle accepted the thesis $\exists y \ \forall x \ (Px \rightarrow Pxy)$ where 'Px' is to be interpreted as 'x is pursued' and 'Pxy' as 'x is pursued for the sake of y'. However, Williams' predicate letters are ambiguous, as he realizes. He asks whether it is a sufficient condition of the truth of 'Pa' that a is at some time pursued by somebody. One might have thought it more natural to take 'Pa' to refer to some particular occasion of pursuit. Williams refuses to resolve the ambiguity. The difficulties, he says, 'lie not so much in the formalization of Aristotle's discussion by means of the predicate 'P' as in Aristotle's discussion itself' (loc. cit. p. 290). But Aristotle's text at this point does not appear ambiguous. He says that happiness is *never* chosen for anything but itself, whereas other things are chosen for the sake of happiness. It is clear that he means not that on some particular occasion honour and pleasure are chosen both for their own sakes and for the sake of happiness, but that on some occasions they are chosen for their own sakes, and on other occasions for the sake of happiness.

We can distinguish between two ways of taking Williams'

[2] E. N. 1102a2 is as multiply ambiguous as 1094a19.

formula. We may take it as saying that on each occasion when something is pursued, it is pursued for the sake of some one thing, namely, happiness. Or we may take it as saying that if something is ever pursued, then it is pursued on at least one occasion for the sake of happiness. Taken in the first way, the formula, as we have seen, would be rejected by Aristotle: pleasure is sometimes pursued for its own sake. I do not see that Aristotle gives us enough information for us to decide what truth-value he would assign to the formula taken in its second sense. Might there not be some things—perhaps, say, some of the perversions listed in Book VII, ch.5—which were sometimes pursued for the sake of pleasure, and never pursued when pleasure was being pursued for the sake of happiness (as by the intemperate man) but only pursued when pleasure was being pursued for its own sake (as by the incontinent man)? There would then be some things which were pursued but never pursued for the sake of happiness. I do not see that Aristotle is committed to ruling out this possibility.

The suggestion that all actions have a single end is one which Aristotle several times considers, but never opts for. At 1097b23 he says that if there is a single end of everything that is done, then this will be *to prakton agathon*, but if there be more than one such end, then it will be these. He at once goes on to say 'there is obviously more than one end', and to exclude from consideration those ends which are not *teleia*, i.e., things such as flutes, wealth, etc., which are always sought in virtue of some other end. But it is not even the case that there is only one *teleion* end: there are some things which are sought both for themselves, and for another end.

In the *Eudemian Ethics* Aristotle says, 'Everyone who has the power to live according to his own choice should dwell on these points and set up for himself some object for the good life to aim at, whether honour or reputation or wealth or culture, by reference to which he will do all that he does, since not to have one's life organized in view of some end is a sign of great folly' (1214b6 ff., quoted Hardie, 277). The fact that this is made as a recommendation shows that what is recommended is not something that is already the case in the behaviour of all men.

It is not true, either in logic or in fact or in Aristotelian doctrine, that all men seek happiness in all they do. Is it even true that all men seek happiness? Here it is useful to follow Hardie in distinguishing between a dominant and an inclusive end. If happiness is thought of as a dominant end, then it is the object of a single prime desire: say, for money, or for philosophy. If it is thought of as an inclusive end, then the desire for happiness is the desire for the orderly and harmonious gratification of a number of independent desires. It seems clear that not everyone has a single dominant aim in life: it is surely possible to lead a life consisting of the successive pursuit of a number of unrelated aims of equal importance. If by happiness we mean something sought as a dominant aim, it seems to be untrue that all men seek happiness.

What of happiness considered as an inclusive aim? It may well be argued that a being who did not plan his life at all, and had absolutely no principles by which he ordered the pursuit of his desires, would be something less than human. But not every inclusive plan of life is a plan for the pursuit of happiness. A man may map out his life in the service of someone else's happiness or for the furtherance of some cause, perhaps devoting his efforts to the pursuit of some end which it may be possible to realize only after his death. Notoriously, such selfless dedication is sometimes the upshot of the wreck of a man's own hopes: he is crossed in love, or loses his family, or sees the collapse of the institutions for which he has worked. '*I* shall never be happy again,' he may think 'but at least I can work for the happiness of others, or seek truth, or help bring about the millennium.' Someone in such a position *has* sought happiness, and so would not be a counter-example to the thesis that all men (at some time or other) seek happiness. But selflessness is not always like this: people may be trained from childhood to pursue an ideal such as the service of the Party, or obedience to God, without this necessarily being presented to them as a means to their own happiness in this life or in another life. A daughter, from the first moment at which she is of an age to manage her own life, may forgo the prospect of marriage and congenial company and creative work in order to nurse a bedridden parent. It is unconvincing to say that such people are seeking their own happiness in so far as they are doing what they want to do. Happiness, considered as an inclusive goal, may include constitutive elements of many different kinds; but not *every* long-term goal consistently pursued is capable of constituting an ideal of happiness. In the cases I have considered happiness is renounced in favour of some other goal; but it is possible to renounce happiness for other reasons also e.g. because the only possible way to achieve one's own happiness may involve the breaking of a promise. In such a case, we might say, the agent must have the long-term goal of acting virtuously: but this would be a goal in a different way from happiness, a goal identified with a certain kind of action, and not a goal to be secured by action.

Aristotle, who considers happiness only in the dominant sense, does not make even the modest claim that everyone seeks happiness. He certainly says that all agree that happiness is the purpose of ethics, and that it is the highest of practical goods. But there is no reason why he should think that everybody practises ethics, or pursues the highest good. All he needs to presume, and all that he does presume, is that all of his lecture audiences are in search of happiness.

Later, Aristotle seeks to show that happiness is identical with philosophic contemplation. Even if he were right about this, it would not, of course, follow that all who seek happiness seek philosophic contemplation. Aquinas, adapting Aristotle, denied that the search for happiness involved any awareness of God. 'Admittedly, man is by nature aware of what by nature he desires, and he desires by nature a happiness which is to be found only in God. But this is not, simply speaking, awareness that there is a God, any more than to be aware of someone approaching is to be aware of Peter, even though it should be Peter approaching: many in fact believe the ultimate good which will make us happy to be riches or pleasure, or some such thing.' This is the phenomenon familiar to logicians as referential opacity.

In Books One and Ten of the *Nicomachean Ethics* Aristotle behaves like the director of a marriage bureau, trying to match his client's description of his ideal partner. In the first book he lists the properties which men believe to be essential to happiness, and in the tenth book he seeks to show that philosophical contemplation, and it alone, possesses to the full these essential qualities. Aristotle's belief that the pursuit of happiness must be the pursuit of a single dominant aim, and his account of the nature of philosophy, seem to be both so seriously mistaken as to make unprofitable a discussion of his arguments that happiness consists in *theoria*. But the properties which he assigns to happiness in the first book are of great interest. They emerge largely negatively from his arguments against inadequate conceptions of happiness.

Aristotle starts from the traditional theme of the three ways of life—the apolaustic, the political, and the theoretic. It is wrong, he says, to think that the life of pleasure is the happy life, for this is brutish. Happiness, then, is to be regarded as a peculiarly human thing. Later on, he expressly denies that animals can be happy, and says that if children are called happy it is only for the hope of happiness which is in them. In English there are idioms in which it is natural to ascribe happiness to animals, but it seems clear that they do not pursue long-term, high-order goals of the kind we have been discussing. But there seems no reason why the pursuit of happiness might not include the pursuit of some things such as health and good food which are benefits which could be enjoyed also by irrational animals. Man differs from other animals in his concern for the absent and the future, and this naturally affects his enjoyment of and attitude to animal goods. Men, unlike animals, suffer from boredom, and human welfare must include some degree of intellectual stimulation and interest. Human happiness, therefore, could not consist wholly in participation of benefits which human beings have in common with non-human animals. But it does not follow, as Aristotle thought, that it must consist wholly in some activity which they do not share at all with other animals.

It seems odd to us that Aristotle should consider happiness an activity at all. He argues that happiness cannot be identical with virtue because it is possible for a man who has virtue to sleep or be idle throughout his whole life, or to suffer great misfortune, and no one would call such a man happy. But surely, if a man spends his whole life in bed and never does any virtuous actions, then it seems at least equally odd to call him virtuous. Happiness seems, like virtue, to be a long-term state rather than a particular activity or career; and if, unlike virtue, it is a state which is vulnerable to misfortune, this is not because it is an activity which is interrupted by misfortune.

Aristotle mentions two other properties of happiness: it must be perfect (*teleion*) and it must be self-sufficient (*autarkes*). Happiness is the most perfect thing: this is something we have already considered, namely, the fact that happiness, unlike wealth and pleasure and reason, is chosen only for its own sake. But there is a difficulty here, for when Aristotle speaks at 1097b2 of honour, pleasure and reason, it looks as if he has in mind once again the three kinds of life. But later he is to identify the life of happiness with the theoretic life. It is odd, then, that *nous* should appear here as something distinct from happiness, and therefore not most perfect, when in Book Ten the theoretic life is going to be praised as most perfect. Perhaps this is just an example of something familiar in recent philosophy: that what appears under one description as a means may appear under another description as an end; as the killing of an enemy may be done *for* revenge and yet be itself the revenge.

The self-sufficiency of happiness, Aristotle says, does not consist in its being a life for a hermit, but rather in its being an activity which by itself, and without anything else, makes life choice-worthy and complete. Of course, other goods added to happiness will add up to something more choice-worthy. This last remark makes it clear that Aristotle did not consider happiness an inclusive state made up of independent goods.

So far we have considered happiness as a goal pursued. So considered, it appears as a long-term, inclusive, comparatively self-regarding goal. Happiness as a realized state cannot be simply identified with the achievement of such a goal; for notoriously a man in pursuit of happiness may realize all the specific goals he has planned and yet not be happy. Happiness as realized appears to be a state of mind, or perhaps rather a state of will: it appears to be akin to contentment and satisfaction, and might perhaps be described as an attitude, were it not that an attitude seems to be something which can be adopted at will in a way in which happiness cannot. Happiness in this sense might seem to be the satisfaction of one's major desires coupled with the belief that such satisfaction is likely to endure. The difficulty in such a definition arises with the word 'major': what is a major desire? It does not seem that we can say that every desire which occupies a great part of an agent's attention and efforts is a major desire in this context; for we might be reluctant to call a man happy whose only concern was to procure heroin, even if he was in a position to obtain regular and safe supplies. On the other hand it does not seem that we can decide *a priori* what a man's major desires must be by considerations of the major needs and concerns of human beings in general. For it seems that a man may be happy in sacrificing his own welfare: many martyrs have died proclaiming their happiness. The pursuit of altruistic goals, I have argued, cannot be called the pursuit of happiness; but the achievement of altruistic goals may bring happiness as a kind of epiphenomenon.

In assessing happiness we have regard not only to the satisfaction of desires, but also to the nature of the desires themselves. The notions of contentment and of richness of life are in part independent, and this leads to paradox in the concept of happiness, which involves both. Plato and Mill sought to combine the two notions, by claiming that those who had experience of both inferior and superior pleasures would be contented only with the superior pleasures of a rich intellectual life. This, if true, might show the felicity of Socrates satisfied, but will not prove that Socrates dissatisfied is happier than a fool satisfied. The greater a person's education and sensitivity, the greater his capacity for the 'higher' pleasures and therefore for a richer life; yet increase in education and sensitivity brings with it increase in the number of desires, and a corresponding lesser likelihood of their satisfaction. Instruction and emancipation in one way favour happiness, and in another militate against it. To increase a person's chances of happiness, in the sense of fullness of life, is *eo ipso* to decrease his chances of happiness, in the sense of satisfaction of desire. Thus in the pursuit of happiness, no less than in the creation of a world, there lurks a problem of evil.

INTELLECT AND IMAGINATION IN AQUINAS[1]

In the first article of question 85 of the First Part of the *Summa Theologiae* St. Thomas affirms that the human intellect understands material things by abstracting from phantasms (*intellectus noster intelligit materialia abstrahendo a phantasmatibus*). My purpose in this paper is to air certain problems in the interpretation of this theory.

Every word in the formula quoted raises a difficulty, not excluding the preposition 'from'. The verb, for instance, is traditionally translated 'understands', but this translation is not beyond question. '*Intelligere*' often does seem to correspond to 'understand' but sometimes it appears a more general verb, like the English 'think'.

In some places Aquinas follows Aristotle in distinguishing two kinds of understanding, two types of intellectual operation. On the one hand there is the understanding of simples (*intelligentia indivisibilium*), and on the other hand there is compounding and dividing (*compositio et divisio*). (See *De Veritate* I, 3; IV, 2; *S.Th.* Ia, 17, 3).

To compound and to divide is to make affirmative and negative judgements (*In I Perihermeneias*, 3). Faced with the content of any proposition, one may either make or withold a judgement about it; if one makes a judgement one may do so truly or falsely, one may do so with or without hesitation, and one may do so on the basis of argument or on grounds of self-evidence. According to various combinations of these possibilities, one's state of mind in relation to the propositional content will be an instance of belief, opinion, doubt, knowledge, or understanding. Whereas

---

[1] In writing this paper I have been influenced by the work of Bernard Lonergan S.J. (*Verbum: Word and Idea in Aquinas*); but I have not adopted the whole of his subtle reconstruction of Aquinas' theory of abstraction.

forming a belief, accepting an opinion, entertaining a doubt, coming to a conclusion, and seeing a self-evident truth are all exercises of the intellectual faculty or understanding, the seeing of self-evident truths is understanding *par excellence* (*De Veritate* XIV, 1). Since Aquinas uses the same verb to refer to the specific activity of grasping self-evidence and as a generic term for various kinds of thought, we cannot tell from the occurrence of the verb alone whether his theory of abstraction is meant as an account of thought in general, or as an account of the grasp of self-evident truths in particular.

St. Thomas observes that any judgement which can be made can be expressed by a sentence (*De Veritate* II, 4). This does not mean that thought is impossible without verbalization for it does not follow that every judgement that *is* made *is* put into words, either orally or in imagination. It does mean, however, that compounding and dividing is the mental analogue of the utterance of affirmative and negative sentences.

The understanding of simples is related to the entertaining of judgements as the use of individual words is related to the construction of sentences. An example of the understanding of simples would be knowledge of what gold is—knowledge of the *quid est* of gold. Such knowledge can be exercised in judgements about gold, and without some such knowledge no judgement about gold would be possible. Some such judgements, such as 'gold is valuable' or 'gold is yellow' require no great understanding of the nature of gold; they presuppose little more than an awareness of what the word 'gold' means. A chemist, on the other hand, knows in a much richer way what gold is. Not only can he list many more of the properties of gold, but he can relate and present those properties in a systematic way, linking them, for instance with gold's atomic number and its place in the periodic table of the elements. The chemist's account of gold would seem to approximate to the ideal described by St. Thomas as knowledge of the quiddity or essence of a material substance (e.g. Ia 3, 3 and 4; 17, 3). In many places St. Thomas observes that one can know what a word 'A' means without knowing the quiddity or essence of A. We know, for instance, what the word 'God' means, but we do not and cannot know God's essence (e.g. *S.Th.* Ia, 2, 2 ad 2). Learning the meaning of a word and acquiring a scientific mastery of the essence of a substance are both exercises of intelligence; but the grasp of essences is understanding *par excellence*. In the case of the understanding of simples, then, no less than in compounding and dividing, we meet a distinction between a broad and a narrow sense of 'understand'. In the broad sense, the acquisition and application of any concept, the formation and expression of any belief count as exercises of the understanding; in the narrow sense, understanding is restricted to insight into essences and the intuition of self-evident truths. Clearly, it is desirable to know whether St. Thomas' theory of abstraction is presented as an account of understanding in the broad sense or of understanding in the narrow sense. If the former, it is a general account of the operation of the intelligence by which language-using human beings surpass dumb animals; if the latter, it is an account of the methodology of *a priori* science. In what follows I shall try to keep both interpretations in mind.

The ambiguity we have noted carries over from the verb *'intelligere'* to the noun *'intellectus'*. The intellect is a capacity, and capacities, as Aquinas frequently observes, are specified by their exercises: to explain the nature of the capacity to φ you must explain what φing is (*S.Th.* Ia 77, 3; 87, 3). The intellect or understanding, being precisely the capacity to understand, cannot be explained without an explanation of what it is to understand. So if 'understand' presents problems, 'intellect' will present analogous problems too. But they are not the only problems presented by Aquinas' theory of abstraction by the intellect.

The intellect, according to St. Thomas, is not one faculty but two: or rather it is a single faculty with two powers: the agent intellect (*intellectus agens*) and the receptive intellect (*intellectus possibilis*). Ia 79, 3 of the *Summa* explains why it is necessary to posit an agent intellect, taking a cue from Aristotle's cryptic dictum in the *De Anima* that there is in the soul one mind for becoming all things and one mind for making all things (III, 430a15).

Plato, St. Thomas says, had no need to posit an agent intellect to make the objects of understanding actually intelligible, because he believed that the forms of material things subsisted without matter and were thus fit objects of understanding, being immaterial *species* or Ideas. But according to Aristotle, there are no forms of things in nature subsisting without matter, and forms existing in matter are not actually intelligible. Consequently, says Aquinas, the natures or forms of perceptible things which we understand need to be made actually intelligible, fit objects of understanding, by some power on the side of the intellect. This is the agent intellect which makes actually intelligible objects of understanding by abstracting *species* from material conditions (*S.Th.* Ia 79, 3).

There is much in this that is difficult to understand: a crucial term is the word transliterated '*species*'. In the passage just summarized it is first used as an expression for Platonic Forms, synonymous with the Latin word 'Idea'. Indeed no English word seems to correspond better to the Latin word '*species*' than the word 'idea'. If the English word is dangerously ambiguous, that is all to the good, since the Latin word is ambiguous in closely parallel ways.

Ideas may be ideas *of* or ideas *that*: the idea of gold, the idea that the world is about to end. Similarly, species may correspond either to the understanding of simples, or to affirmation and negation. (See, for example, *S.Th.* Ia IIae, 55, 1). For *species*, in one sense, are dispositions of the human intellect (Ia IIae, 50, 4), and to the two types of intellectual activity correspond two types of dispositional properties of the intellect. If the two types of activity are interpreted in the broad sense, as the acquisition and application of concepts, and as the formation and expression of beliefs, then the two types of dispositions, the two types of *species*, will be the concepts and beliefs themselves. To have the *species* corresponding to the proposition that p will be to have the belief that p; to have the *species* of A will be to have the concept of A, to have the ability to think of A.

In summary fashion, we might say that for Aquinas ideas include both concepts and beliefs. But here we meet a further ambiguity: for in contemporary philosophy 'concept' has two contrasting uses. In one sense, which we might call the Wittgensteinian sense, a concept is something subjective: to possess a concept is to possess a certain skill, for instance to have mastered the use of a word (e.g. *Philosophical Investigations*, I, 384). It was in this sense that the word was used in the preceding paragraph. But in another sense, which we might call the Fregean, concepts are something objective. For Frege a concept is the reference of a predicate. In the sentence 'Eclipse is a horse', according to Frege, just as the name 'Eclipse' stands for a horse, so the predicate '. . . is a horse' stands for a concept—and a concept is not something in anyone's mind, but a particular type of function, a function whose value for every argument is a truth-value (*Philosophical Writings*, trs. Geach–Black, 43, 59). To this objective use of 'concept' there corresponds an objective use of '*species*', to refer not only to Platonic ideas, which Aquinas rejected, but also to Aristotelian forms, which he accepted. It is in this sense that Aquinas can say that *species* are the objects of the intellect's activity (Cf. *ScG*, II, 73).

More commonly, however, Aquinas says—as in the quotation from which we began—that what the intellect understands, the object of the intellect, is (the nature of) material things. A material thing, according to Aristotelian hylemorphism, is composed of matter and form; an individual man such as Peter is a parcel of matter bearing the form of humanity. Aquinas, in opposition to Plato, often insists that there is not in the world any humanity as such, or Ideal Man; there is only the humanity of Peter, the humanity of Paul, and so on (*S.Th.* Ia 84, 4). The humanity, or human nature, of Peter would be an instance of what Aquinas calls 'a form existing in matter'—something in his terminology 'intelligible' (because a form), but not 'actually intelligible' (because existing in matter). Humanity in the abstract is actually intelligible, but humanity in the abstract is nowhere to be found; humanity in matter is found wherever there are men, but humanity in matter is as such no fit object for the mind. It is to bridge this gap that the agent intellect is necessary. Presented with humanity in matter, the agent intellect creates the intellectual object, humanity as such. In what way is it presented with humanity in matter? 'In phantasms' Aquinas replies; and for the moment we may paraphrase this as 'in experience'.

Let us try to present this doctrine in non-hylemorphic terms. In order to possess a concept of something which can be an object of an experience, it is not sufficient simply to have the appropriate experience. Young children see coloured objects before they painfully acquire colour-concepts; dumb animals can see and taste a substance such as salt but they cannot acquire the concepts which language-users can exercise in general judgements about salt. A special ability unshared by animals is necessary if human beings are to acquire concepts from the experience which they share with animals. Animals share with human beings the experience of pain, and human beings *feel* pains from birth if not before; but as Wittgenstein observed we acquire the *concept* 'pain' when we learn language (loc. cit.). Again, rats can see, and discriminate between circles and triangles; but no amount of gazing at diagrams will make a rat a student of geometry. The specifically human ability to acquire complicated concepts from experience, and to grasp geometrical truths presented in diagrams, will perhaps be what Aquinas has in mind when he speaks of the agent intellect.

Contrasted with the agent intellect, there is the receptive intellect (*intellectus possibilis*). The receptive intellect is the power to exercise the dispositions acquired by the use of the agent intellect. 'One and the same soul' we are told 'in so far as it is actually immaterial, has a power called the agent intellect which is a power to make other things actually immaterial by abstracting from the conditions of individual matter, and another power to receive ideas of this kind, which is called the receptive intellect as having the power to receive such ideas' (*S.Th.* Ia 79, 4 ad 4). The receptive intellect is, St. Thomas says, the *locus* of *species*, the storehouse of ideas (*S.Th.* Ia 79, 6, esp. ad 1.). Varying the metaphor, the receptive intellect is the unwritten tablet, the *tabula rasa*, of which Aristotle wrote (*De Anima* III, 430a1). As concepts and beliefs are acquired through the operation of the agent intellect upon experience, the tablet becomes covered with writing, the empty storehouse fills up with ideas. To find out the contents of a man's receptive intellect at a given time you must find out what he understands, what he knows, what he believes at that moment. In fact the *intellectus possibilis* of a man may be thought of as the collection of concepts and beliefs that he possesses: it is his mind in the sense in which we speak of the contents of a mind.

Frequently Aquinas speaks of the receptive intellect in hylemorphic terms. As prime matter is to the forms of sense-perceptible objects, so the receptive intellect is to all ideas. Prime matter is matter which as such is not any particular kind of stuff; not that there is any matter which is stuff of no particular kind, but that matter, *qua* matter, is not stuff of any particular kind, and can be stuff of any kind whatever. Similarly, the receptive intellect does not, as such, contain any particular ideas, but can contain any idea whatever: 'to begin with it is in potentiality to all such ideas' (*S.Th.* Ia 84, 3). True to his hylemorphism, Aquinas prefers the language of *informing* to that of *containing*: the intellect is *informed* with various *species* (*S.Th.* Ia 79, 6). We use the same metaphor, oblivious of its hylemorphic background, when we speak of being informed upon a topic, or acquiring information about it.

According to hylemorphic theory, to acquire the form of F-ness is to become F: thus, to acquire the form of redness is to become red, just as to possess the form of humanity is to be a man. If we treat an idea, then, as a form informing the intellect, it seems that we must say that the intellect becomes F when it is informed by the idea of F-ness. This, then, will be why Aristotle said that there was in the soul a mind for becoming everything, and that the mind when it understands becomes different things in turn (*De An.* III, 430a15; cf. *S.Th.* Ia 79, 6).

What can we make of this strange conclusion? St. Thomas says that as physical matter has potentialities which are realized by perceptible *esse*, so the receptive intellect has potentialities which are realized by mental *esse* (Ia IIae, 50, 4). Commenting on this passage, I once wrote as follows:

> A leaf may be now green and now brown; when it was green it had a potentiality of being brown which is realized when it is brown; the 'is' in 'is brown' stands for an *esse* which is perceptible *esse*, the *esse* of *being brown*. Now it is clear that a man's capacity to think is realized when he thinks a particular thought; but it is not as if we could say that a man thinking of a horse *is* a horse, or even *is* intelligibly a horse, so why does St. Thomas speak of *esse* here? Perhaps the answer is to be sought on these lines. The history of a man's intellect is the history of the thoughts he has, and at any given moment there is nothing actual which makes a man a thinking being other than the thought he is thinking. In this sense, my intellect is my present thought of a horse, a thought which is capable of changing into a thought of anything else whatever. Now if we think of 'a thought of a horse' as meaning the same as 'a horse in thought' we can say that the intellect of a man, who is thinking of a horse, is a horse in thought. Generalizing, then, we can say that if a man is thinking of X, his intellect is X-in-thought; and further, that no matter what X may be, a human intellect *can* be X-in-thought. This last conclusion, reached in a roundabout fashion, I take to be a more or less literal translation of '*Intellectus habet potentiam ad esse intelligibile*' (*Summa Theologiae*, Blackfriars edition, XXII, 40–41).

I now think that this is misleading in several ways. In the first place, what St. Thomas means by the information of the receptive intellect by an idea is not the episodic exercise of a concept in the thinking of a particular, dated, thought; but rather the acquisition of the lifetime or at least long-term capacity to think thoughts of a certain kind. The exercise of such a capacity is not itself a form but is an activity proceeding from the form: to adapt St. Thomas' standard illustration, it is related to the form as the activity of heating the kettle is related to the form of heat possessed by the stove. For a stove to be hot is, *inter alia*, for it to be able to heat the kettle; for me to possess the concept *round* is for me to be able, *inter alia*, to reflect that the earth is round (Ia IIae, 50, 4; 51, 3).

Secondly, it is not part of St. Thomas' theory that the intellect, when it acquires the concept *horse*, becomes a real horse, or even, strictly speaking, becomes an immaterial horse. The concept *horse*, being applicable to any horse, is not the concept of any particular horse. It is not the concept of an immaterial horse either, for it is part of the concept of a horse that a horse should be a material object. A horse, being a material object, must have a certain size and mass; and this, too, is part of the concept *horse*, that a horse should have a certain size and mass. But there is no particular size or mass which a horse *qua* horse must have, and so no particular size or mass belongs to the concept. St. Thomas makes a similar point.

> There are two kinds of matter: common matter, on the one hand, and designated or individual matter on the other. Common matter is e.g. flesh and bone; individual matter is e.g. this flesh and these bones. Now the intellect abstracts the idea of a natural thing from individual perceptible matter, but not from common perceptible matter: it abstracts, for instance, the idea of *man* from this flesh and these bones, which do not belong to the concept but are parts of the individual . . . but the idea of *man* cannot be abstracted by the intellect from flesh and bone as such (*S.Th.* Ia 85, 1 ad 1).

If, then, the receptive intellect when informed by the species of F-ness becomes F, the receptive intellect does not become a real horse, but an abstract horse; and an abstract horse is not something, on Aquinas' theory, which exists anywhere outside the mind.

Thirdly, my observation that one thought may turn into another thought was not to the point. For the analogy between prime matter and the receptive intellect stands in need of a qualification which St. Thomas himself makes at Ia 84, 3 ad 2. Prime matter, he says, has its substantial *esse* through form—for matter to exist is for it to be F—and there cannot be existent matter which has no form.

But the receptive intellect does not have its substantial *esse* through its ideas: the intellect of a new-born baby exists though it has no ideas; consequently the ideas which inform the intellect are accidental forms (like the form of heat in water) rather than substantial forms (like the form of horse or man). And when St. Thomas follows Aristotle in describing the mind as *becoming* its object, the becoming must be thought of as the acquisition of a new characteristic (like *becoming red*) rather than as the turning into a new kind of thing (like *becoming a butterfly*).

The restriction on the analogy between prime matter and the receptive intellect occurs in the course of an attack on the doctrine of innate ideas: and it is in contrast to that doctrine that Aquinas' own theory of abstraction is worked out. Plato had maintained, Aquinas says, that the human intellect naturally contained all intelligible ideas, but was prevented from using them because of its union with the body. Against this Aquinas marshals both empirical and metaphysical arguments.

> If the soul has a natural knowledge of all these things it does not seem possible that it should so far forget this natural knowledge as to be ignorant that it has it at all. For nobody forgets what he naturally knows, as that the whole is greater than its parts and so on. Plato's theory seems especially unacceptable if the soul is, as maintained above, naturally united to the body; for it is unacceptable that the natural operation of a thing should be altogether impeded by something else which is also natural to it. Secondly, the falsity of this theory appears obvious from the fact that when a certain sense is lacking, there is lacking also the scientific knowledge of things perceived by that sense. A blind man, for instance, cannot have any knowledge of colours. This would not be the case if the

soul's intellect were naturally endowed with the concepts of all intelligible objects (*S.Th.* Ia 84, 3).

Later, Aquinas praises Aristotle for taking a middle course between the innate idealism of Plato and the crude empiricism of Democritus.

> Aristotle maintained that the intellect had an activity in which the body had no share. Now nothing corporeal can cause an impression on an incorporeal thing, and so, according to Aristotle, the mere stimulus of sensible bodies is not sufficient to cause intellectual activity. Something nobler and higher is needed, which he called the agent intellect: it makes the phantasms received from the senses to be actually intelligible by means of a certain abstraction (*S.Th.* Ia 84, 6).

In what sense, on Aquinas' account, are concepts *abstracted from* phantasms? Principally, there appear to be two separable doctrines united in the theory. The first is that concepts and experiences stand in a certain causal relation; the second is that they stand in a certain formal relation.

The causal relation is spelt out in the continuation of the passage just cited.

> In this way, then, intellectual activity is caused by the senses on the side of the phantasm. But since phantasms are not sufficient to affect the receptive intellect unless they are made actually intelligible by the agent intellect, sense-knowledge cannot be said to be the total and complete cause of intellectual knowledge, but only the material element of its cause.

To say, then, that concepts are abstracted from experience is to say at least that experience is a necessary causal condition for the acquisition of concepts. How far this is true seems to be partly an empirical matter and partly a philosophical question. It is an empirical matter, for instance, to discover how much a blind man might learn of a textbook on optics. It is a philosophical question how far mastery of such a textbook could count as 'possession of the science of colour' without e.g. the ability to match colours against colour samples.

Besides having a causal relation to experience, Aquinas' ideas have a formal relation to them: that is, concepts on his theory are abstract *in comparison with* experiences. Sense-experience, he believed, is always of a particular individual; intellectual knowledge is primarily of the universal (Ia, 86, 1). Consequently, intellectual concepts can be said to abstract from much that is included in sense-experience. This is the sense of 'abstraction' that is spelt out in the passage from which this paper began (*S.Th.*Ia, 85, 1).

> It is peculiar to (the human intellect) to know form existing individually in corporeal matter but not *as* existing in such matter. But to know that which is in individual matter but not *as* in such matter is to abstract the form from the individual matter which the phantasms represent.

In answer to an objector, Thomas goes on to clarify.

> What belongs to the specific concept (*pertinet ad rationem speciei*) of any material thing such as a stone, or a man, or a horse, can be considered without the individual characteristics which are not part of the specific concept. This is what it is to abstract the universal from the particular, or the intelligible idea from the phantasms, namely, to consider the specific nature without considering the individual characteristics which are represented by the phantasm (Ibid. ad 1).

This formal relation is distinct from the causal relation, for what Aquinas says here would be true even if universal concepts were not acquired from experience. Even innate ideas would still be more abstract than representations of individuals, whether these latter were themselves acquired or innate. For to have the concept of man is not to be able to recognize or think of a particular man with particular characteristics. It is *inter alia* to be able to recognize any man no matter what his particular characteristics, to think about men without necessarily attributing particular characteristics to them, and to know general truths about man as such. And this is true no matter how the concept has been acquired.

In modern philosophy there is a familiar, if no longer popular, theory that the acquisition of universal concepts can be explained by selective attention to features of particular experience. One version of the theory was ridiculed by Berkeley in *The Principles of Human Knowledge* (8 ff.), another was treated by Wittgenstein in *Philosophical Investigations*. Wittgenstein writes:

> When someone defines the names of colours for me by pointing to samples and saying 'This colour is called "blue", this "green" . . .' this case can be compared in many respects to putting a table in my hands, with the words written under the colour-samples.—Though this comparison may mislead in many ways.—One is now inclined to extend the comparison: to have understood the definition means to have in one's mind an idea of the thing defined, and that is a sample or picture. So if I am shown various different leaves and told 'This is called a "leaf"', I get an idea of the shape of a leaf, a picture of it in my mind.—'But what does the picture of a leaf look like when it does not shew us any particular shape, but "what is common to all shapes of leaf"? Which shade is the "sample" in my "mind" of the colour green—the sample of what is common to all shades of green?
>
> But might there not be such "general" samples? Say a schematic leaf, or a sample of pure green?' Certainly there might. But for such a schema to be understood as a *schema*, and not as the shape of a particular leaf, and for a slip of pure green to be understood as a sample of all that is greenish and not as a sample of pure green,—this in turn resides in the way the samples are used (I, 74).

Aquinas' language in his last quoted passage might make it look as if he held a theory such as Berkeley and Wittgenstein criticized. But in fact this appears unlikely. First of all, the theory described by Wittgenstein demands that an idea be treated quite seriously as a mental *picture*. St. Thomas speaks of ideas as being likenesses of the things which are thought of by their aid, and this has sometimes led people to think that he was talking of mental images. But according to his terminology mental images seem rather to be phantasms; and phantasms are sharply distinguished from ideas. Phantasms, he says, come and go from day to day, but ideas remain for life; the image of one man differs from the image of another, but both are recognized as men by one and the same idea or *species* (*ScG*, II, 73 and 78).

Moreover, the 'mental sample' view of abstraction leaves no room for the task Aquinas assigns to the agent intellect. When Aquinas talks of the need for the agent intellect to make the phantasms actually intelligible, he seems to be making the same point as Wittgenstein is making when he says that even a schematic sample has to be understood *as a schema* if it is to help us to understand what a leaf is. Indeed Aquinas expressly rejects the idea that a concept is just a mental image shorn of inessential features.

> Through the power of the agent intellect and through its attention (*conversio*) to the phantasms, there results in the receptive intellect a certain likeness which is a representation of the things whose phantasms they are, but only in respect of their specific nature. It is thus that the intelligible concept is said to be abstracted from the phantasms; it is not that numerically the same form, which was at one time in the phantasms, later comes into the receptive intellect, in the way in which a body may be taken from one place and transferred to another.

This is confirmed when Aquinas contrasts the abstraction made by the intellect with that made by the senses. For even the senses, he explains, do abstract in a way.

> A sense-perceptible form is not in the same manner in the thing outside the soul as it is in the sense-faculty. The sense-faculty receives the forms of sense-perceptible things without their matter, as it receives the colour of gold without the gold; and similarly the intellect receives the ideas of bodies, which are material and changeable, in an immaterial and unchangeable fashion of its own (*S.Th.* Ia 84, 1).

The less materially a faculty possesses the form of the object it knows, Aquinas explains, the more perfectly it knows: thus the intellect, which abstracts the ideas not only from matter but also from material individuating characteristics, is a more perfect cognitive power than the senses, which receive the form of what they know without matter but not without material conditions (Ia 84, 2). Perceptible qualities outside the soul are already actually perceptible; but since there are no Platonic ideas, there is nothing outside the soul actually intelligible corresponding to material objects (Ia 79, 3 ad 1).

Aquinas frequently insists that phantasms play a necessary part not only in the acquisition of concepts, but also in their application. During our mortal life, he says, 'it is impossible for our intellect to perform any actual exercise of understanding (*aliquid intelligere in actu*) except by attending to phantasms.' He offers two proofs of this thesis. First, although the intellect has no organ of its own, the exercise of the intellect may be impeded by injury to the organs of imagination (as in frenzy) or of memory (as in amnesia). Such brain damage prevents not only the acquisition of new knowledge, but also the utilization of previously acquired knowledge. This shows that the intellectual exercise of habitual knowledge requires the co-operation of imagination and other powers. Secondly, he says, 'everyone can experience in his own case that when he tries to understand something, he forms some phantasms for himself by way of examples in which he can so to speak take a look at what he is trying to understand.' Similarly 'when we want to make someone understand something, we suggest examples to him from which he can form his own phantasms in order to understand' (Ia 84, 7).

A metaphysical reason is offered to explain this. The proper object of the human intellect in the human body is 'the quiddity or nature existing in corporeal matter'. The quiddities of corporeal things must exist in corporeal individuals.

> Thus, it is part of the concept of a stone, that it should be instantiated in a particular stone, and part of the concept of a horse, that it should be instantiated in a particular horse, and so on; so the nature of a stone or of any material thing cannot be completely and truly known unless it is known as existing in the particular; but the particular is apprehended by the senses and the imagination. Consequently, in order to have actual understanding of its proper object, the intellect must turn to phantasms to study the universal nature existing in the particular (Ia, 84, 7).[2]

[2] As it is more than usually difficult to provide an untendentious translation of this passage, I give the original. *De ratione naturae lapidis est, quod sit in hoc lapide; et de ratione naturae equi est, quod sit in hoc equo: et sic de aliis. Unde natura lapidis, vel cuiuscumque materialis rei cognosci non potest complete, et vere, nisi secundum quod cognoscitur ut in particulari existens: particulare autem apprehendimus per sensum et imaginationem. Et ideo, necesse est, ad hoc quod intellectus*

Several things are noteworthy about this whole argument. First, it starts from the premise that there is no bodily organ of the intellect. One might be inclined to ask: how does St. Thomas know that brain activity is not necessary for thought, even for the most abstract and intellectual thought? Second, these two possible lines of answers suggest themselves. The first is that St. Thomas would agree that there is not in fact, in this life, any thought, however exalted, which is not accompanied by brain activity. But he would say that this was precisely because there was no thought, however exalted, which is not accompanied by the activity of the imagination or the senses. The second is that even if brain activity is a necessary condition for thought, this does not make the brain an organ of thought in the way that the eyes are the organ of sight and the tongue and palate are organs of taste. An organ is, as its etymology suggests, something like a tool, a part of the body which can be voluntarily moved and used in characteristic ways which affect the efficiency of the discriminatory activity which it serves. The difficulty is that these two answers seem to cancel out. In the sense of 'organ' in which there is no organ of thought, there is no organ of imagination either—I cannot move my brain in order to imagine better in the way that I can turn my eyes to see better—and in the sense in which the brain is an organ of the imagination there seems no good reason to deny that it is an organ also of the intellect.

Again, the second argument seems to concern rather the first acquisition of understanding than its later utilization. This is so whether we think of St. Thomas as having in mind the production of diagrams (as when in the *Meno* Socrates taught the slave-boy geometry) or the construction of fictional illustrations (as when Wittgenstein imagines primitive language-games in order to throw light on the workings of language). It does not seem to be true that whenever concepts are exercised there must be something going on, even mentally, which is rather like the drawing of a diagram or the telling of a detailed story.

Despite all this, it does seem true in one sense that there must be some exercise of sense or imagination, some application to a sensory context, if one is to talk at all of the exercise of concepts or the application of the knowledge of necessary truths. For a

actu intelligat suum obiectum proprium, quod convertat se ad phantasmata, ut speculetur naturam universalem in particulari existentem.

man to be exercising the concept, say, of red, it seems that he must be either discriminating red from other colours around him, or having a mental image of redness, or a mental echo of the word 'red', or be talking, reading, or writing about redness, or something of the kind. He may indeed be able to *possess* the concept *red* without this showing in his experience or behaviour on a given occasion, but it seems that without some vehicle of sensory activity there could be no *exercise* of the concept on that occasion. Similarly with the knowledge of a general truth, such as that two things that are equal to a third are equal to each other. For this knowledge to be exercised it seems that its possessor must either enunciate it, or apply it say in the measurement of objects, or utilize it in some other way even if only in the artful manipulation of symbols.

This seems both true and important, but the nature of Aquinas' arguments for his thesis makes it doubtful whether he understood it in this sense. It is true that he does say that the phantasm employed in the exercise of the concept of A need not be the phantasm of A itself. But when he says this he has in mind particular cases where A is something immaterial and to that extent unpictureable (*S.Th.* Ia 74, 7 ad 3). Whereas it seems that for it to be the case that every exercise of a concept involved attention to a phantasm, it would rarely be the case that the phantasm attended to was a representation of the object of the concept.

Attention to phantasms (*conversio ad phantasmata*) is, according to Aquinas, something which is necessary for every exercise of every concept, whether in general or particular judgements. But uses of general concepts in judgements about perceptible particulars presented him with a special problem: the judgement, for instance, that this tomato is red, that these particular objects matching a single standard match each other. Aquinas thought that it was the sensory context which gave the judgement its particular reference; and this view has recently been defended by Geach (*Mental Acts*, 65 ff.). In expounding Aquinas, however, Geach appears to misrepresent his position. 'Aquinas'expression', he writes, 'for the relation of the "intellectual" act of judgement to the context of sense-perception that gives it a particular reference was *conversio ad phantasmata*'. But *conversio ad phantasmata*, as we have seen, is needed for all judgements, and not just for judgements about particulars; and for the special relation to sensory context involved in judgements about particulars Aquinas uses a different metaphor and speaks of reflection on sense-appearances, *reflexio supra phantasmata*.³ This is introduced at *S.Th.* 86, 1, in answer to the question whether our intellect knows particulars. The answer reads as follows.

> Our intellect cannot directly and primarily know particular material things. The reason is that the principle of individuation in material things is individual matter: but as was said above, our intellect understands by abstracting intelligible ideas from such matter. What is abstracted from individual matter is universal, and so our intellect is directly capable of knowing only universals. But indirectly and by a kind of reflection it can know individuals, because as was said above even after it has abstracted intelligible ideas, it cannot exercise them in acts of understanding without turning to phantasms. . . . Thus, by means of its ideas it directly understands the universal, and indirectly the particulars of which the phantasms are phantasms; and thus it forms this proposition, *Socrates is a man* (Ia 86, 1).

Exactly what is meant by 'reflection' is and remains obscure in Aquinas' writings, and I shall not attempt to investigate it here. But I must turn to the overdue task of interpreting the notion of *phantasm*. There are many passages in Aquinas, some of which have been quoted, where translations such as 'sense-appearances' or 'sense-impressions' suggest themselves (e.g. *S.Th.* Ia, 74, 6). But in other places it seems, as one would expect, that phantasms are produced by the *phantasia* or imagination. This, we are told, is the locus of forms which have been received from the senses as the receptive intellect is the locus of ideas (*S.Th.* Ia 78, 4). These forms, we are told, may be reshuffled at will to produce phantasms of anything we care to think about: we can for example combine the form which represents Jerusalem and the form which represents fire to make the phantasm of Jerusalem burning (*De Veritate*, XII, 7). This makes a phantasm appear to be something like a mental image. But if we accept this interpretation, then it seems that St. Thomas

³ On the distinction between *conversio* and *reflexio*, see Lonergan, *Verbum*, 159 ff.

is wrong in saying that phantasms are particular in the way sense-impressions are. I cannot see a man who is no particular colour, but I may have a mental image of a man without having a mental image of a man of a particular colour, and I may imagine a man without being able to answer such questions as whether the man I am imagining is dark or fair. Imagination differs from sensation in another way which makes it misleading to combine the two under a single rubric such as 'phantasm'. It is not possible to be mistaken about what one is imagining in the various ways in which it is possible to be mistaken about what one is seeing: a man's description of what he imagines enjoys a privileged status not shared by his description of what he sees. There are some passages in which St. Thomas seems to suggest that whenever we see something we have at the same time a phantasm of what we see; and sensory illusions are explained by saying that the senses themselves are not deceived, but only the *phantasia* on which they act (*In IV Met*, lect. 14). It seems implausible to suggest that whenever we see a horse we have at the same time a mental image of a horse. Perhaps the theory is that if we see accurately our phantasm of a horse is a sense-impression; if we are mistaken about what we see, and there is no horse there at all, then our phantasm is a mental image. This theory seems to be confused in several ways, but it is hard to be sure whether St. Thomas held it or not.

Certainly St. Thomas is prepared to call the imagination a *sense*: sight, hearing, etc. are outer senses, the memory and the imagination are inner senses. This suggests an unacceptable assimilation. We can see some reason for calling the imagination a sense if we reflect that the power to have visual imagery depends on the ability to see. But this was not St. Thomas' reason for calling the imagination a sense, because he thought that this dependence was not a matter of logic but a contingent fact (*De Veritate*, XII, 7). In fact he thought that the inner senses resembled the outer senses in having particular objects and bodily organs. As we have seen, both these points of resemblance seem in fact to be lacking. Consequently it is difficult to accept Aquinas' theory of the inner senses, and in particular of the imagination, without modification.

This has important consequences not only for his theory of abstraction but also for the whole problem of the relations between mind and body. In the course of a polemic against Averroes, Aquinas had occasion to raise the question: what makes an individual's ideas *his* ideas (Ia 76, 1 and 2)? Clearly, there need be nothing in the content of a belief held by one man to distinguish it from a belief held by others. Innumerable people besides myself believe that $2+2=4$: when I believe this, what makes the belief *my* belief? Aquinas' answer, in effect, is that my beliefs are beliefs of the soul which is individuated by my body, and because they are acquired and employed with the aid of phantasms generated by my brain (Ia IIae, 50, 4). This answer seems to lead to an account of the relationship between mind in body which is fundamentally as dualistic as that of Descartes. For it follows, and St. Thomas himself drew the conclusion, that the body is necessary for intellectual activity not in order to provide the mind with an instrument, but only to provide the mind with an object —phantasms being, in one sense of the word 'object', the object of the intellect's activity. (See Aristotle, *De Anima* 1, 403a8 ff., and St. Thomas' commentary). If this is a correct account then my body is no more essentially concerned in my thought than Leonardo is concerned in my looking at the Mona Lisa. This is what enables St. Thomas to say that thought is an activity of the soul alone, and thus that the soul, having an independent activity, is capable also of independent existence, as an incorruptible substance in its own right (*S.Th.* Ia 75, 6).

The question 'What makes my thoughts *my* thoughts?' has an oddly contemporary ring. It would perhaps be rash to think that contemporary studies have provided an answer to the question; but they have certainly shown one direction in which to look for an answer. My thoughts, surely, are the thoughts which find expression in the words and actions of *my body*. If we are to make progress with such perennial problems as 'can my thoughts outlast my body?' it seems that we must investigate the relation between thought and its expression in linguistic and non-linguistic behaviour. It is a weakness of St. Thomas' philosophy of mind that he has very little to say about this relation.

DESCARTES ON THE WILL

The problems I wish to discuss concern two developments which took place, or are alleged to have taken place, in Descartes' teaching concerning the relation of the intellect and the will.*

The first is this. In the *Regulae* (AT X, 420) Descartes says that we must distinguish the faculty of the intellect by which it intuits and knows things from the faculty by which it makes affirmative and negative judgements.[1] In the same book he says that belief in revelation, by contrast with science, 'is not an act of the mind but of the will'.[2] On the other hand, in the *Principles of Philosophy* we are told that, while sensation, imagination, and pure intellection are modes of perception, desire and aversion, affirmation, denial and doubt are different modes of willing.[3] This classification of affirmative and negative judgements as an act of will is anticipated in the Fourth Meditation, where he distinguishes the intellect or faculty of knowing (*facultas cognoscendi*) from the will or faculty of choosing (*facultas eligendi*) and says that the intellect merely perceives ideas for judgement[4] and that judgements are acts of the will;[5] the cause of erroneous judgement is the fact that our will extends further than our intellect.[6]

In the same passage of the *Meditations* occurs the sentence

---

* References are given to the volume and page of the standard edition of Descartes' works, *Oeuvres de Descartes*, ed. Ch. Adam et P. Tannery, 12 Vols., Paris, 1897–1910 (henceforth cited as AT). I have made use eclectically of the translations by Haldane and Ross and by Geach and Anscombe.

[1] *Distinguamus illam facultatem intellectus per quam res intuetur et cognoscit ab ea qua judicat affirmando vel negando.*
[2] *Non ingenii actio sit sed voluntatis* (AT X, 370).
[3] *Sentire imaginari et pure intelligere sunt tantum modi percipiendi; ut et cupere aversari, affirmare, negare, dubitare sunt diversi modi volendi* (AT VIII, 17).
[4] *Per solum intellectum percipio tantum ideas de quibus iudicium ferre possum* (AT VII, 50).
[5] *Illos actus voluntatis, sive illa iudicia, in quibus fallor* (AT VII, 60).
[6] *Latius pateat voluntas quam intellectus* (AT VII, 50).

which introduces the second of the two contrasts I want to discuss. 'I could not refrain from judging' Descartes says 'that what I so clearly understood was true . . . because from a great light in my intellect there followed an inclination of will.'[7] The assertion that the will is determined by the intellect is generalized in the geometrical exposition of the *Meditations* which follows the Second Objections. 'The will of a thinking substance is impelled—voluntarily and freely, since that is of the essence of the will, but none the less infallibly—towards a good clearly known to it.'[8] And in the reply to the same objections he gives examples of propositions which are so clearly perceived by the intellect that we cannot think of them without believing them to be true (AT VII, 145). In a letter perhaps written to Mesland in 1645, on the other hand, Descartes wrote as follows. 'It is always open to us to hold back from pursuing a clearly known good, or from admitting a clearly perceived truth, provided we consider it a good thing to demonstrate the freedom of the will by so doing.'[9]

We have, then, two contrasts. In the *Regulae*, Descartes treats judgement as an act of the intellect; in later works he treats it as an act of the will. In the *Meditations* Descartes says that clear perception determines the will; in the letter to Mesland he says that clear perception can be rejected by the will. I want to take each of these contrasts in turn to see how far they represent a real change of mind in Descartes.

I. *Descartes' Theory of Judgement*

To the modern philosopher, the statement of the *Regulae* that judgement is an act of the intellect, seems more natural than the theory of the *Principles* that judgement is an act of the will. A practical judgement, a decision what to do, may perhaps be regarded as an act of the will; but a speculative judgement, a decision that such and such is the case, an assent to a proposition

---

[7] *Non potui non iudicare illud quod tam clare intelligebam verum esse . . . quia ex magna luce in intellectu magna consequuta est propensio in voluntate* (AT VII, 59).
[8] *Rei cogitantis voluntas fertur, voluntarie quidem et libere—hoc enim est de essentia voluntatis—sed nihilominus infallibiliter, in bonum sibi clare cognitum* (AT VII, 166).
[9] *Semper enim nobis licet nos revocare a bono clare cognito prosequendo, vel a perspicua veritate admittenda, modo tantum cogitemus bonum libertatem arbitrii nostri per hoc testari* (AT VI, 197).

rather than to a proposal: this seems, if we are to talk of faculties at all, to belong to a cognitive rather than to an appetitive faculty. Such too was the opinion of the scholastics of Descartes' time. To see what he is likely to have been taught by the Thomists of La Flèche, we may consider the following text of St. Thomas, one of many quoted in Gilson's *Index Scolastico-Cartesien*. In Ia IIae, 17, 6 St. Thomas inquires whether the act of reason can be commanded by the will. He replies as follows. 'Since reason reflects on itself, it can order its own acts just as it can order the acts of other faculties; and so its own act can be commanded. But it must be observed that the act of reason can be considered in two ways. First we may consider the exercise of the act: in this sense the act of reason can always be commanded, as when someone is told to pay attention and use his reason. Secondly, we may consider the object of the act; and in this connection there are two different acts of reason to be considered. The first is the apprehension of truth about something: this is not in our power but comes about in virtue of a natural or supernatural light; and so in this respect the act of reason is not in our power and cannot be commanded. But there is another act of reason which consists in assent to what is apprehended. Where what is apprehended is something like the first principles to which the intellect naturally assents, to assent or dissent is not in our power but in the order of nature; and so, strictly speaking, it is at the command of nature. But there are some things apprehended which do not so convince the intellect as to take away its power of assent or dissent; these leave it free at least to suspend its assent or dissent for some cause; and in such cases assent and dissent are in our power and subject to command.'[10]

[10] *Respondeo dicendum quod quia ratio supra seipsam reflectitur, sicut ordinat de actibus aliarum potentiarum, ita etiam potest ordinare de suo actu; unde etiam actus ipsius potest esse imperatus. Sed attendendum est quod actus rationis potest considerari dupliciter: uno modo quantum ad exercitium actus, et sic actus rationis semper imperari potest, sicut cum indicitur alicui quod attendat, et rationi utatur. Alio modo quantum ad objectum, respectu cujus duo actus rationis attenduntur: primo quidem, ut veritatem circa aliquid apprehendat; et hoc non est in potestate nostra; hoc enim contingit per virtutem alicuius luminis vel naturalis vel supernaturalis. Et ideo quantum ad hoc actus rationis non est in potestate nostra, nec imperari potest. Alius autem actus rationis est, dum his quae apprehendit assentit. Si igitur fuerint talia apprehensa, quibus naturaliter intellectus assentiat, sicut prima principia, assensus talium vel dissensus non est in potestate nostra, sed in ordine naturae; et ideo, proprie loquendo, naturae imperio subjacet. Sunt autem quaedam apprehensa, quae non adeo convincunt intellectum, quin possit assentire vel dissentire, vel saltem assensum vel dissensum suspendere propter aliquam causam; et in talibus assensus vel dissensus in potestate nostra est, et sub imperio cadit.*

Any reader of Descartes will notice great similarities between his doctrine and that of St. Thomas. Descartes distinguishes frequently between what we perceive or understand and what we judge: out of many passages, we can quote the letter to Hyperaspistes; 'I have frequently observed that what men judge to be the case differs from what they really understand to be the case'.[11] Descartes' distinction between perception and judgement corresponds to Aquinas' between apprehension and assent. Like Aquinas, Descartes thinks that there are some truths which are perceived in such a way as to force assent; Aquinas calls these first principles, Descartes calls them clear and distinct perceptions. As he wrote to Regius in 1640: our mind is of such a nature that it cannot fail to assent to what is clearly understood.[12] Like Aquinas, Descartes thinks that in other cases the mind is free to assent or dissent; but whereas Aquinas says that assent or dissent in such a case is at the command of the will, Descartes as we have seen regards assent as being, not just commanded by the will but as itself an act of the will. I know of no scholastic prior to Descartes who held this view, and I am unimpressed by the attempts of Gilson and Koyré to find precedent for it in Augustine, Thomas and Scotus.[13]

When he wrote the *Regulae*, Descartes still held the orthodox Thomist view, as we have seen. There is, it is true, one passage which Leslie Beck sees as presupposing the later view 'that judgement whether in its pure or practical use is an assent or dissent, an act of will'.[14] But the passage is most naturally interpreted as applying only to practical matters. Descartes exhorts us, in studying, 'to think solely of increasing the natural light of reason,

---

[11] *Frequenter animadverti ea quae homines iudicabant ab iis quae intelligebant dissentire* (AM V, 52).
[12] *Mens nostra est talis naturae, ut non potest clare intellectis non assentiri* (AT III, 64).
[13] Koyré quotes a passage from Augustine in which a judgement is attributed to the will; but this concerns the act of faith, and not regular speculative judgement (*Essai sur l'idée de Dieu et les preuves de son existence chez Descartes*, Paris, 1922, p. 78).
Gilson's best text for the assimilation between St. Thomas and Descartes is the following:
Conclusio syllogismi quae fit in operabilibus ad rationem pertinet, et dicitur sententia vel iudicium, quam sequitur electio; et ob hoc ipsa conclusio pertinere videtur ad electionem tanquam ad consequens.
This is far from Descartes' identification of judgement and election; and in any case applies only to practical reasoning (*in operabilibus*) (S. Th. Ia IIae, 13 1 ad 2).
[14] L. J. Beck, *The Method of Descartes* (Oxford, 1952), p. 17.

not with a view to solving this or that scholastic problem but in order that in all the happenings of our life, our intellect may show our will what alternative to choose'.[15] In this passage it is choice, and not judgement, not even practical judgement, which is attributed to the will; though if Descartes had called the choice following deliberation 'judgement' he would not have been departing from scholastic usage.[16] So *pace* Beck, the *Regulae* do not differ from the Thomist doctrine that judgement is an act of the intellect.

Some time, then, between 1628 and 1640 Descartes changed his mind about the nature of judgement. It is not easy to discover when or why he did so. The *Discourse on Method* is not helpful: it hardly mentions the will. In the Third Section, while urging the importance of following men's practice rather than their preaching, Descartes observes that many people do not know what they really believe. 'For the mental act of believing a thing is different from the act of knowing that one believes it; and the one act often occurs without the other.'[17] In his commentary Gilson cites here a passage from Regis: 'According to Descartes, the mental act by which we judge something to be good or bad is a function of the will, and the action by which we know that we have judged thus is a function of the intellect. It is no wonder if two functions, one of the intellect and one of the will, are different and can occur apart.'[18] Regis' annotation shows that what is here said is coherent with Descartes' mature theory of judgement; but it does not establish that he already held it. First of all, the passage concerns practical and not speculative judgement; secondly, even someone who thinks that both belief and the knowledge that one believes

---

[15] *Cogitet tantum de naturali rationis lumine augendo, non ut hanc aut illam scholae difficultatem resolvat, sed ut in singulis vitae casibus intellectus voluntati praemonstret quid sit eligendum.*

[16] *Iudicium est quasi conclusio et determinatio consilii. Determinatur autem consilium primo quidem per sententiam rationis, et secundo per acceptationem appetitus . . . et hoc modo ipsa electio dicitur quoddam iudicium a quo nominatur liberum arbitrium* S. Th. I, 84 3 ad 2.

[17] *L'action de la pensée par laquelle on croit une chose, étant differente de celle par laquelle on connait qu'on la croit, elles sont souvent l'une sans l'autre* (AT VI, 23).

[18] *Exactement commenté par Pierre-Silvain Regis*: '*Car il faut savoir que, selon M. Descartes, l'action de l'esprit par laquelle nous jugeons qu'une chose est bonne ou mauvaise est une fonction qui appartient à la volonté, et que l'action par laquelle nous connaissons que nous avons jugé ainsi est une fonction qui appartient à l'entendement. Ou, ce n'est pas une grande merveille que deux fonctions, dont l'une appartienent à l'entendement et l'autre à la volonté soient differentes, et que l'une puisse être sans l'autre.*' Gilson, op. cit., p. 238.

are acts of the intellect can think it possible for one of them to occur without the other.[19]

We may turn next to Descartes' unpublished writings for a clue in this matter. In 1630 in letters to Mersenne Descartes put forward his famous doctrine of the creation of the eternal truths. It was the common scholastic doctrine that the truths of logic and mathematics were necessary in such a way that not even God could change them; they were not altogether independent of him, because they depended for their truth upon his essence or nature; but they did not depend on his free will in the way that the existence of the world did. Descartes argued that the scholastics talked of God 'as if he were Jupiter or Saturn, subject to Styx and Fate': in contrast he insisted that it is God who has established these laws in nature just as a King establishes laws in his kingdom. The eternal truths 'are true or possible because God knows them as true or possible; they are not, contrariwise, known to God as true as though they were true independently of him ... in God knowing and willing are but one thing; so that from the very fact of his willing something he knows it, and for this reason alone is such a thing true'.[20]

Attempts have been made to find sources for this doctrine in Scotus and Ockham; like the attempts to find scholastic precedents for the theory of judgement, they are unconvincing.[21] Both the doctrine of the creation of eternal truths and the theory that judgement is an act of the will are, of course, examples of a 'voluntarist' tendency—a tendency to attribute to the will (human or divine) things which might be attributed to something else (the intellect, or the nature); and such a tendency is to be found in Scotus and Ockham (the happiness of the blessed resides primarily in the will; good and evil are as they are because God so wills). But the resemblance seems to end there. And the connection, if there is one, between the two Cartesian doctrines, is fairly tenuous. It is true that if in God knowing and willing two and three to make

---

[19] The difficulty is to reconcile what Descartes says here with *Passions*, article I, 19.
[20] *Sunt tantum verae aut possibiles quia Deus illas veras aut possibiles cognoscit, non autem contra veras a Deo cognosci quasi independenter ab illo sint verae ... en Dieu ce n'est qu'un de vouloir et de connaître; de sorte que ex hoc ipso quod aliquid velit, ideo cognoscit, et ideo tantum talis res est vera* (AT I, 149).
[21] There is no real evidence for Koyré's view that Descartes read Scotus in the 1620s. Even according to Koyré, Scotus held only that God could change moral laws such as the decalogue, not logical or mathematical truths.

five is one and the same act, then we have an act which can be regarded as at the same time an act of the intellect and of the will. But that this is the case with God, whose nature is simple and undivided, does not tell us anything about what is the case in man where intellect and will are distinct. Descartes does not even use the word 'judgement' about God in this context, though no doubt if he did, he would say that in God judging, just like willing and creating, was identical with seeing, knowing or understanding.

Mersenne informed Descartes that his doctrine resembled that of the Oratorian P. Gibieuf, who published in 1630 his *De Libertate Dei et Hominis*. Descartes, on receiving the book from Mersenne (cf. AT I, 153, 174, 220) had pleasure, as Baillet says, to find wherewithal to authorize what he conceived of indifference and free will. But though Gibieuf's views on the liberty of God, and on the Jesuit doctrine of liberty of indifference, were very close to those of Descartes, there is nothing in his *De Libertate* to suggest that speculative judgement is an act of the will. On the contrary, the book reaffirms the traditional doctrine on this point. 'It is to be observed that liberty is an appetitive, not a cognitive faculty; because it is a faculty whose object is the end or the supreme good, which is an object of appetite not of intellect. It is no objection to this that it is called the faculty of free decision or judgement, and that judgement or decision is an act of reason. For it is called the faculty of free decision, both because it is moved by the free decision or judgement, and because free decision or judgement, when it is perfect and, as they say, practico-practical, includes its acceptance; not that its actual act is a judgement or decision.'[22]

Altogether, I can find no passage in Descartes' letters prior to the writing of the *Meditations* which clearly teaches that judgement is an act of the will. This makes it the more surprising that when it is put forward there it is not presented as a novel thesis which needs to be argued for, but is presupposed and applied before being stated in so many words. Only Gassendi seems to

[22] *Observandum secundo, libertatem esse facultatem appetitivam, non cognoscitivam: quia est facultas cuius objectum est finis, sive summum bonum, quod est appetitus non intellectus. Nec refert quod vocetur facultas liberi arbitrii sive iudicii, iudicium autem sive arbitrium sit actus rationis. Vocatur enim facultas liberi arbitrii, tum quia movetur a libero arbitrio sive iudicio, tum quia liberum arbitrium sive iudicium (quando perfectum est et practice practicum, ut vocant) eius iam acceptationem includit; non autem quod actus eius elicitus sit iudicium ipsum sive arbitrium* (op. cit., 355).

G

have objected, and that not in his first objections, but in his Instances, of which one is thus summarized: 'To avoid confusion the intellect and the will should be so distinguished that whatever concerns cognition and judgement should be attributed to the intellect, and whatever concerns appetition and choice should be attributed to the will.'[23]

Being unable to find a historical source from which Descartes might have borrowed the doctrine that judgement is an act of the will, we must ask what philosophical considerations may have led him to devise it for himself. The one which first suggests itself is the fact that judgement, even speculative judgement, is, often at least, a voluntary matter. What we believe is influenced by our desires; rash judgement or stubborn incredulity is blamed as a moral fault; courage and effort may be required to retain rational conviction in face of emotional pressures. In the controversy with Regius there is some evidence that this consideration was the origin of Descartes' theory. In the *Notes on a Programme*, Descartes objects to Regius' dividing understanding into perception and judgement. 'I however saw that, over and above perception, which is required in order that we may judge, there must needs be affirmation or negation to constitute the form of judgement, and that it is often possible for us to withhold our assent, even if we perceive a thing. I attributed the act of judging, which consists solely in assent, that is in affirmation or negation, not to the perception of the understanding, but to the determination of the will.'[24]

In his doctoral thesis, *La doctrine Cartésienne de la liberté*, Etienne Gilson argued, on the basis of this and other texts, that the origin of Descartes' theory of judgement was to be sought in his desire to adapt Aquinas' theodicy to his own purposes. The problem of evil presented itself to Descartes above all as the problem of error. There existed a set of arguments in Aquinas to show how God could be exonerated from blame for human sin.

---

[23] *Vitandae confusionis gratia debere intellectum et voluntatem ita distingui ut quicquid cognitionis et judicii est, ad intellectum pertineat; quicquid appetitionis electionisque, ad voluntatem* (AT VII, 404).

[24] *Ego enim, cum viderem, praeter perceptionem, quae praerequiritur ut iudicemus, opus esse affirmatione vel negatione ad formam iudicii constituendam, nobisque saepe liberum esse ut cohibeamus assensionem, etiamsi rem percipiamus: ipsum actum iudicandi, qui non nisi in assensu, hoc est, in affirmatione vel negatione consistit, non retuli ad perceptionem intellectus, sed ad determinationem voluntatis* (AT VIIIa 363).

By making judgement an act of the will, Descartes assimilated erroneous judgement to sinful volition. Thus he was able to use Aquinas' arguments to exonerate the author of nature from blame for human fallibility. 'The problem of sin is the theological form of the problem of error and the problem of error is the philosophical form of the problem of sin.'[25]

Two objections may be made to Gilson's thesis, one sound and the other unsound. The unsound objection runs as follows. It is just not the case that all judgement is voluntary in the sense of being avoidable. There are many judgements, as Descartes is the first to admit, that we cannot help making. Even the *Notes on a Programme* merely say '*nobis* saepe *liberum esse ut cohibeamus assensionem*', and it appears disingenuous for Gilson to paraphrase this, as he does, '*nous savons par expérience que cette affirmation et cette négation sont* toujours *en notre pouvoir*' (op. cit., p. 276).

This objection is unsound because Descartes does not consider it necessary for a judgement to be voluntary that it should be avoidable. Like most scholastics, Descartes was willing to call an act voluntary if it was in accordance with the agent's desires, whether or not it was avoidable; indeed, unlike most scholastics, he was prepared to call an unavoidable, but welcome, action 'free' as well as 'voluntary' (AT IV, 116).[26] Moreover, it is undoubtedly true, as Gilson says, that in the Fourth Meditation Descartes does use in the interest of theodicy arguments very parallel to those of Aquinas.

The crucial objection to Gilson's thesis is that it was not necessary, for Descartes to be able to exploit Aquinas' arguments, that he should have made judgement an act of the will; it was sufficient for him to make it a voluntary act of the intellect. In scholastic terminology, he did not need to regard judgement as an *actus elicitus voluntatis*; it was perfectly sufficient for him to regard it, as Aquinas himself did, as an *actus imperatus a voluntate*.[27] Not all voluntary acts are acts of the will: walking, for

---

[25] '*La problème du péché est la forme théologique de celui de l'erreur et la problème de l'erreur est la forme philosophique de celui de la péché* (op. cit., p. 284).
[26] Moreover any erroneous judgement was for Descartes voluntary in the sense of avoidable.
[27] Descartes does not, so far as I know, use the pair *actus elicitus/actus imperatus*. But he frequently uses the terminology of eliciting acts (e.g. Med. IV, AT VII, 60; N. in P, AT VIIIa, 363) and the terminology of *actus imperatus* is implied in the letter 463.

instance, may be a voluntary act but it is an act of the body rather than of the will. Descartes might reject this example because, as he says often, nothing is completely in my power but my thoughts (e.g. *Discourse*, Part III; letter 154). But imagination and intellectual thought are under the control of will—we can decide what we are going to think about—but are not acts of the will. 'Our desires are of two sorts: one of which consists in the actions of the soul which terminate in the soul itself, as when we desire to love God, or generally speaking, apply our thoughts to some object which is not material. . . . When our soul applies itself to imagine something which does not exist, as when it represents to itself an enchanted palace or a chimera, and also when it applies itself to consider something which is only intelligible and not imaginable, e.g. to consider its own nature, the perceptions which it has of these things depend principally on the act of will which causes it to perceive them.' Such perceptions, then are voluntary; but they are perceptions of the intellect, not inclinations of the will (*Passions*, articles 18, 20). The problem we might say is not that error belongs to philosophy and sin to theology; it is that the object of the intellect is truth, and that of the will is goodness; that error is a matter of falsehood, and sin of badness. And this problem Gilson's theory is impotent to solve.

Put in less scholastic terms, the problem is why, and with what justification, Descartes should lump judgement together with desire and aversion and separate it from perception and imagination. One reason might be that judgement and desire are, on Descartes' theory, the only acts which we perform if and only if we want to perform them. Walking is something which we do only if we want to; but not every time we want to walk do we succeed in walking. If we want to imagine something, on the other hand, we succeed in doing so; but we often have thoughts in our imagination which we do not will to be there. Neither of walking nor imagination, therefore, is it true that they are acts which we perform if and only if we want to. Judgement and desire, of which this is true, are therefore voluntary in a special way.

But there is a further reason for regarding judgement as an act of the will: and light may be thrown on this from an unexpected quarter. In modern times Frege has taught us to make a sharp distinction between the sense of a sentence which remains the same whether a sentence appears as a complete unit of communication or as a hypothetical clause in a longer sentence, and the assertion of a sentence which he marked by a special sign whose function was to indicate that the reference or truth-value of what follows it is 'the true'.[28] Many other writers have followed Frege, notably R. M. Hare, who in *The Language of Morals* made a distinction in sentences between a *phrastic* (which contains the descriptive content of the sentence) and a *neustic* (which marks the mood of a sentence, and of which Frege's assertion sign would be an example).[29] The two sentences 'You will shut the door' and 'You, shut the door' have something in common—the state of affairs which would verify the prediction is the same as the state of affairs which would constitute obedience to the command, namely your shutting the door. But as sentences in different moods they differ; and the similarity and differences might be brought out by rephrasing them

> Your shutting the door in the immediate future, please.
> Your shutting the door in the immediate future, yes.

It is not difficult to see a similarity between Descartes' theory of judgement and the theory of Frege and Hare. The perceptions of the intellect, it might be said, are concerned with the unasserted phrastics; an affirmative judgement is as it were the mental attachment of the neustic 'yes' to the phrastic presented by the intellect, the mental attachment of the assertion sign to the Fregean 'sense' which is the object of perception. There is of course the difference that neither Frege nor Hare has a negative neustic; negation is regarded not as the polar opposite of assertion, but as the assertion of a phrastic with a negative sense, containing within itself the logical constant for negation.

In two passages Descartes seems to make the contrast between phrastic and neustic in the scholastic terminology of matter and form. In the Third Meditation, having said that only those of his thoughts that are like pictures really deserve the name of 'idea', he goes on to say 'Other thoughts have other forms in addition:

---

[28] *The Philosophical Writings of Gottlob Frege*, ed. Geach and Black (Oxford, 1952), pp. 62ff.
[29] *The Language of Morals* (Oxford, 1952), pp. 18ff. In his more recent work Hare distinguishes what he called a neustic into neustic, tropic and clistic. These refinements are not necessary for a comparison with Descartes, who does not make any analogous distinctions.

when I will, am afraid, assert, or deny, there is always something which I take as the subject of my thought; but my thought comprises more than the likeness of the thing in question; of these some are termed volitions or emotions, others are termed judgements'.[30] The word 'subjectum' suggests to a modern reader the translation 'topic'; but in fact it is used in scholastic terminology as a synonym for 'materia' in contrast to 'forma', which is explicitly used to refer to what differentiates a judgement from a pure idea.[31]

In this passage judgements are contrasted with volitions rather than classified as a species of volition; this makes clear that Descartes uses 'volition' in a narrow sense as well as a broad sense, volitions strictly so called being a species of a genus of acts of will which includes also judgements.[32] In the other passage which uses scholastic terminology we are told very explicitly that judgement is an act of the will. This is in the passage already quoted from the *Notes on a Programme*, where Descartes is objecting to Regius' classification of mental phenomena. 'Then he divides what he calls the intellect into perception and judgement, which does not accord with my view. I observed that besides the perception which was required for judgement there must also be an affirmation or negation to constitute the form of judgement; and that it is often open to us to withhold our assent even if we perceive a thing. And so I attributed the act of judging, which consists purely in assent, i.e. affirmation and negation, not to the perception of the intellect, but to the determination of the will' (AT VIII 303).

The statement that the intellect is concerned with the un-

---

[30] *Aliae vero alias quaedam praeterea formas habent; ut cum volo, cum timeo, cum affirmo, cum nego, semper quidem aliquam rem ut subjectum meae cogitationis apprehendo, sed aliquid etiam amplius quam istius rei similitudinem cogitatione complector; et ex his aliae voluntates, sive affectus, aliae autem iudicia appellantur* (AT VII, 37).

[31] Cf. also II replies: *distinguendum est inter materiam sive rem ipsam cui assentimur, et rationem formalem quae movet voluntatem ad assentiendum.*

[32] On the basis of this passage Brentano argued that Descartes did not really regard judgement as an act of the will at all; he explains away Principle 32 and the *Notes on a Programme* by saying that Descartes means judgement is an *actus imperatus voluntatis* and not an *actus elicitus voluntatis*. He does not seem to have noticed that in the Fourth Meditation Descartes speaks of '*eliciendos illos actus voluntatis, sive illa iudicia, in quibus fallor*' (AT VII, 60). The French makes even clearer the identity of the act of the will and the judgements: '*Dieu concourt avec moi pour former les actes de cette volonté, c'est à dire les jugements dans lesquels je me trompe*' (AT IX, 48). See Brentano, *The True and the Evident* (London, 1966), pp. 28–32.

asserted phrastics needs some qualification; for Descartes uses 'intellect' no less than 'will' in two senses. In one sense the intellect is the possession of the power to recall and combine ideas; it is in this sense that every judgement presupposes an act of the intellect, since judgements must concern ideas, neustics must be attached to phrastics. In another sense the intellect is the faculty which produces clear and distinct ideas and intuits their truth; it is in this sense that Descartes can explain error by saying that the faculty of judging extends farther than the faculty of understanding. He explained this to Gassendi in the Fifth Replies (AT VII, 376). 'When you judge that the mind is a rarefied body, you can understand that it is a mind, that is, a thinking thing, and you can understand that a rarefied body is an extended thing; but you do not understand that one and the same thing is both thinking and extended; this is something you merely will to believe because you believed it before and you do not like changing your mind. When you judge that an apple, which happens to be poisoned, is suitable food, you understand that its odour and colour etc. are pleasant, but not that it is a good thing for you to eat; but because you want it so, you judge it so. And so I agree that we do not will anything about which we understand nothing at all; but I deny that we understand as much as we will; because we can, about one and the same thing, will much and know very little.'[33]

The ambiguity of Descartes' 'intellectus' can be paralleled in the English word 'understanding' which is the nearest word to Descartes' French 'entendement'. When we use the word 'understanding', like Locke, as a name for a very general faculty, we might say that the belief that eighteen is a prime number is an operation of the understanding; but of course in another sense no one can understand that eighteen is a prime number since it is not. So, in this passage of the reply to Gassendi, Descartes restricts the verb 'intelligere' to his adversary's correct performances

---

[33] *Ita cum iudicas mentem esse tenue quoddam corpus intelligere quidem potes, ipsam esse mentem, hoc est, rem cogitantem, itemque tenue corpus esse rem extensam; unam autem et eandem esse rem quae cogitat et quae sit extensa, profecto non intelligis, sed tantummodo vis credere, quia iam ante credidisti nec libenter de sententia decedis. Ita cum pomum, quod forte venenatum est, iudicas tibi in alimentum convenire, intelligis quidem eius odorem, colorem, et talia grata esse, non autem ideo ipsum pomum tibi esse utile in alimentum; sed quia its vis, ita iudicas. Atque sic fateor quidem nihil nos velle de quo non aliquo modo intelligamus; sed nego nos aeque intelligere et velle; possumus enim de eadem re velle permulta et perpauca tantum cognoscere* (AT VII, 377).

—understanding what mind is, and what body is—and refuses to apply it to his mistaken idea that mind is a kind of body.

There is a difference between phrastics and the 'materia' of Descartes' judgements in that phrastics are unambiguously composite, propositional, containing argument and function; whereas the matter of Cartesian judgement is ideas, and ideas may be simple (e.g. the idea *of* mind) or composite (e.g. the idea 'horse with wings') and composite ideas seem sometimes to be expressed nominally (idea *of* a horse with wings) and sometimes propositionally (idea *that* a horse has wings). Sometimes Descartes writes as if even a non-propositional idea can be asserted; whereas of course it would be impossible to attach a neustic to a name standing alone. In such a case, presumably the assertion amounts to the assertion of an extra-mental existence of the thing represented by the idea.[34]

The work of the intellect in the strict sense involves not only the understanding of ideas but also seeing the combination between ideas (as, that thought is linked with existence). The intellect, in the wide sense, includes the imagination, whose function is to combine together the ideas of various bodily objects (forming say, the idea of a goat-stag out of the idea of a goat and the idea of a stag). But it is not clear, in Descartes' system, what faculty is responsible for linking together non-corporeal ideas which do not belong together in reality: e.g. what links the ideas together in the idea that mind is a rarefied body? In Gassendi, one might think, it is the will that links these ideas together, just as it is the will which judges the composite idea so formed to be true. But this will not apply in the case of Descartes, whose will makes no such judgement, and who yet in order to reject the judgement has to put the two ideas together in the sentence 'The mind is not a rarefied body'.

The comparison between Descartes' perceptions and Hare's phrastics, then, though illuminating, needs qualification. Let us now turn to the other element, the neustic. Does a consideration of this throw any light on why Descartes considered judgement an act of the will? If the command 'Jones shut the door' can be rewritten 'Shutting of the door by Jones, please', it seems that

---

[34] Cf. Third Meditation, AT VIII, 33; and the letter to Mersenne, no. 308, in which Descartes says that all ideas not involving affirmation or negation are innate.

Jones' acceptance of, or assent to, this command, might be expressed by 'Shutting of the door by Jones, yes'. Elsewhere I have suggested that wishes, desires and other pro-attitudes could be similarly expressed artificially by a unit consisting of a phrastic describing the approved state of affairs, and a neustic indicating the attitude of approval.

Now of course when Jones agrees to the order 'shut the door' by saying 'yes', he means 'yes I will', not 'yes that is the case'. None the less, it is a striking fact that we can give an affirmative response not only to propositions and questions, but also to commands and projects, by the same word 'yes'. Our attitudes to both assertions and proposals may be described in terms of affirmation and negation; both may be characterized as 'assent' or 'dissent'; both as forms of commitment. Assent to both a proposition and a proposal may be sincere or insincere, rash or cautious, right or wrong.

It is this, I think, which provides the main justification for Descartes' treatment of judgement as an act of the will. For what is it, after all, to ascribe particular actions to one or other faculty? It is to group those actions together in virtue of common features of description and assessment which apply to them. If we take together all those mental activities which can have rightness or wrongness ascribed to them, we will find that they include all those activities which Descartes ascribed to the will and exclude those which he ascribed to the intellect.

But this justification of Descartes' procedure suggests immediately an objection to it. It may be wrong to think that the earth is larger than the sun, and wrong to have vengeful desires; but the wrongness in the one case consists in falsehood and in the other case in evil. The right, we might say grandly, is a genus of which the species are the true and the good; and Descartes' classification emphasizes the unity of the genus at the cost of ignoring the diversity of the species.

It would be open to Descartes to make the following reply. It is indeed the case that judgement, unlike desires, can be classified as true or false. But it is not true that judgements cannot be classified as good and evil. Believing that the human mind, properly used, was infallible, Descartes believed that every erroneous judgement was a moral fault. 'What theologian or philosopher' he asked 'or indeed what rational man has ever denied that we are in less danger of error the more clearly we understand something before assenting to it, and that it is a sin to make a judgement before the case is known?'[35] Moreover, the truth and falsehood which belongs to a judgement, Descartes might have said, belongs to it not in so far as it is an assent, but in so far as what is assented to—what is presented by the intellect—corresponds or does not correspond to reality. Erik Stenius has pointed out that unasserted phrastics possess a truth-value independently of being asserted; what is contained in an if-clause, for example, either is or is not a description of what is the case, even though, since it occurs in an if-clause, it is not being put forward as such a description.[36] This is a fact which is presupposed in the truth-tabular definition of the logical constants. The truth of assertions might be regarded as parasitic on this: an assertion is true if and only if what is asserted is true, i.e. is a description which corresponds to reality.

In fact Descartes does not answer along these lines. Instead he says: 'Ideas considered in themselves and not referred to something else, cannot strictly speaking be false; whether I imagine a she-goat or a chimera, it is not less true that I imagine the one rather than the other. Again, falsehood is not to be feared in the will or the emotions; I may desire what is evil, or what does not exist anywhere, but it is none the less true that I desire it. Only judgements remain: it is here that I must take precautions against falsehood.'[37] This, as I have remarked elsewhere, is a strange argument.[38] One could as well argue that judgements in themselves could not be false, on the grounds that whether what I judge is true or false, it is none the less true that I judge. I think this reveals a genuine confusion in Descartes. His theory of judgement involves an important insight which he failed to follow up.[39]

[35] *Quis unquam vel Philosophus vel Theologus, vel tantum homo ratione utens non confessus est eo minori in errandi periculo nos versari, quo clarius aliquid intelligimus, antequam ipsi assentiamur, atque illos peccare qui causa ignota iudicium ferunt* (II Replies, AT VII, 147).
[36] *Wittgenstein's 'Tractatus'* (Ithaca, N.Y., 1960), p. 165 ff.
[37] *Quod ad ideas attinet, si solae in se spectentur, nec ad aliud quid illas referam, falsae proprie esse non possunt; nam sive capram, sive chimaeram imaginer, non minus verum est me unam imaginari quam alteram. Nulla etiam in ipsa voluntate, vel affectibus, falsitas est timenda; nam quamvis prava, quamvis etiam ea quae nusquam sunt, possim optare, non tamen ideo non verum est illa me optare. Ac proinde sola supersunt iudicia, in quibus mihi cavendum sit ne fallar* (AT VII, 37).
[38] *Descartes* (New York, 1968), p. 117.
[39] A further example of the same confusion occurs in the reply to Gassendi: *Cum autem prave iudicamus, non ideo prave volumus, sed forte pravum quid; nec*

The point which Descartes has missed is what we may call—to adapt an expression of J. L. Austin's—the *onus of match*.[40] If we express assent to a proposition or a project in the phrastic-neustic form, each expression will contain a description of a possible state of affairs, plus an assent-indicator. But let us suppose that the possible state of affairs does not, at the relevant time, obtain. Do we fault the assent, or the state of affairs? Do we condemn the original assent as a false assertion, or do we complain about the subsequent state of affairs as an unsatisfactory outcome? Elsewhere, I have tried to clarify this point by considering the different relation of an architect's plan, and a plan in a guidebook, to a building. 'If the building and the plan do not agree, then if the plan is in a guidebook, it is the 'plan which is wrong; if the plan was made by an architect, then there is a mistake in the building.'[41] In the relation between the guidebook and the building, the onus of match is on the plan; in the relation between the architectural drawing and the building, the onus of match is on the building. So, in general, in assenting to a proposition, we place an onus on a phrastic to match the world; in assenting to a command or project we place an onus on something non-linguistic (primarily, our own actions) to match a phrastic.

Descartes, in lumping together affirmation and desire, negation and aversion, confounds the different onus of match involved in the two different kinds of assent and dissent. This, it seems to me, is the fundamental defect in his theory of judgement as an act of the will. The absence of the notion of onus of match at this point is the more surprising as a very similar notion plays a fundamental part in Descartes' moral theory. 'My third maxim was to try always to conquer myself rather than fortune; to change my desires rather than the order of the world' (*Discourse*, part 3).

II. *The Evolution of Descartes' Doctrine of Freedom*

Throughout the history of philosophy there have been two contrasting methods of expounding the nature of human free will.

---

quidquam prave intelligimus, sed tantum dicimur prave intelligere, quando iudicamus nos aliquid amplius intelligere quam revera intelligamus (AT VII, 377).
[40] 'How to Talk', *Philosophical Papers*, p. 190.
[41] 'Practical Inference', *Analysis* 26.3.68. The point was first made by Miss Anscombe (*Intention*, p. 56), who modestly but incorrectly attributes it to Theophrastus.

The first is in terms of power: we are free in doing something if and only if it is in our power not to do it. The second is in terms of wanting: we are free in doing something if and only if we do it because we want to do it. This is the distinction which Hume made when he urged us to distinguish 'betwixt the liberty of spontaneity, as it is call'd in the schools, and the liberty of indifference; betwixt that which is oppos'd to violence, and that which means a negation of necessity and causes' (*Treatise*, III, II, II). Liberty defined in terms of wanting is liberty of spontaneity; liberty defined in terms of power is liberty of indifference. As Hume observed, the former, but not the latter, is compatible with causal determinism.

In their accounts of human freedom most philosophers have combined both elements and Descartes is no exception. In the Fourth Meditation we read 'Freewill consists simply in the fact that we are able alike to do and not to do a given thing (that is, can either assert or deny, either seek or shun); or rather, simply in the fact that our impulse towards what our intellect presents to us as worthy of assertion or denial, as a thing to be sought or shunned, is such that we feel ourselves not to be determined by any external force'.[42] This appears tantamount to saying 'Free will consists in liberty of indifference, or rather in liberty of spontaneity'. One immediately wants to ask: what is the force of the 'or rather' here? Does it mark second thoughts, so that Descartes is withdrawing the statement that freewill consists in liberty of indifference and replacing it with the more correct statement that it consists in liberty of spontaneity? Or does it mean that liberty of indifference, properly understood, is identical with liberty of spontaneity so that the '*vel potius*' means something like 'or, in other words'? The answer, I think, is not quite either of these: it is rather that Descartes thinks that free will often does consist in liberty of indifference, but that sometimes it consists only in liberty of spontaneity, and that is all that is essential to it. He goes on: 'There is no need for me to be impelled both ways in order to be free; on the contrary, the more I am inclined one way—either because I clearly understand it under the aspect of truth and goodness, or because God has so disposed my inmost conscious-

[42] *Voluntas, sive arbitrii libertas, . . . tantum in eo consistit quod idem vel facere vel non facere—hoc est affirmare vel negare, prosequi vel fugere—possimus, vel potius in eo tantum quod ad id quod nobis ab intellectu proponitur affirmandum vel negandum, sive prosequendum vel fugiendum, ita feramur, ut a nulla vi externa nos ad id determinari sentiamus* (AT VII, 57).

ness—the more freely do I choose that way.'[43] In this passage there is a difficulty in the translation of the phrase 'in utramque partem ferri posse'. If this is taken to mean 'there is no need for me to be able to go both ways'—i.e. to *act* either way—then the sentence contains an outright denial that liberty of indifference is necessary for free will. Geach, however, takes the passive sense of *ferri* seriously, and translates 'there is no need for me to be impelled both ways'—i.e. to have reasons on both sides. Taken this way, the sentence is not incompatible with the view that liberty of indifference is essential to genuine freedom; for a full-blooded liberty of indifference would be a freedom to act either way even though the reasons for acting might be all on one side.

I think that Geach's rendering is correct: it is borne out by the French version of the Duc de Luynes which, we are told, was revised by Descartes himself. This reads 'Il n'est pas nécessaire que je sois indifférent a choisir l'un ou l'autre des deux contraires'. At first sight this too looks like a denial of the need for liberty of indifference: but in fact when Descartes uses the word 'indifference' he does not mean what Hume and the scholastics meant by indifference. This point is made explicitly in the correspondence with Mesland which we shall consider later; but it is clear enough from what follows in the *Meditations*. 'The indifference that I am aware of when there is no reason urging me one way rather than the other, is the lowest grade of liberty.'[44] But the indifference which is the balance of reasons is not the indifference which is the ability to act either way. The present text does not by itself tell us whether Descartes believed such an ability to remain when all the reasons are on one side. 'If I always saw clearly what is good and true, I should never deliberate as to what I ought to judge or choose; and thus, although entirely free, I could never be indifferent.'[45] The fact that I would not have to deliberate ('je ne serais jamais en peine de délibérer' as the French has it) if I always saw

---

[43] *Neque enim opus est me in utramque partem ferri posse, ut sim liber, sed contra, quo magis in unam propendeo, sive quia rationem veri et boni in ea evidenter intelligo, sive quia Deus intima cogitationis meae its disponit, tanto liberius illam eligo.*
[44] *Indifferentia illa, quam experior cum nulla me ratio in unam partem magis quam in alteram impellit, est infimus gradus libertatis.*
[45] AT VII, 58: *si semper quid verum et bonum sit clare viderem, nunquam de eo quod esset iudicandum vel eligendum deliberarem; atque ita, quamvis plane liber nunquam tamen indifferens esse possum.*

what was good does not establish that I would always *do* what was good. So the indifference which is here said to be inessential to freedom is the indifference which consists in the balancing of reasons and not the indifference which is the ability to act either way.

However, shortly afterwards, in the case of the *cogito* Descartes expressly denies that such an ability exists. 'I could not but judge to be true what I understood so clearly; not because I was compelled to do so by any external cause, but because the great illumination of my understanding was followed by a great inclination of the will; and my belief was the more free and spontaneous for my not being indifferent in the matter.'[46] A truth so clearly seen, then, cannot but be judged to be the case; so the ability not to judge, which in this case would constitute liberty of indifference, is lacking. Where there is no such clarity, however, indifference remains and this is true not only where there are no reasons, or equal reasons, on either side, but wherever the reasons on one side fall short of certainty. For the thought of their uncertainty itself constitutes a reason on the other side. 'However much I may be drawn one way by probable conjectures, the mere knowledge that they are only conjectures and not certain and indubitable reasons is enough to incline my assent the other.'[47] God, we are told, has 'given me the liberty to assent or not to assent to things of which he put no clear and distinct perception in my understanding'.[48]

The Fifth Meditation and the Second Replies make clear that God has given me no such liberty in cases where I do have clear and distinct perception. 'There are some things which are so clear and simple that we cannot think of them without believing them to be true.'[49] The Seventh Axiom, quoted earlier, says 'The will of a thinking thing is impelled, voluntarily of course and

---

[46] *Non potui quidem non iudicare illud quod tam clare intelligebam verum esse; non quod ab aliqua vi externa fuerim ad id coactus, sed quia ex magna luce in intellectu magna consequuta est propensio in voluntate, atque ita tanto magis sponte et libere illud credidi, quanto minus fui ad istud ipsum indifferens* (AT VII, 59).

[47] *Quantumvis enim probabiles conjecturae me trahant in unam partem, sola cognita quod sint tantum conjecturae, non autem certae atque indubitabiles rationes, sufficit ad assensionem meam in contrarium impellendam.*

[48] *Mihi libertatem dederit assentiendi vel non assentiendi quibusdam, quorum claram et distinctam perceptionem in intellectu meo non posuit* (AT VII, 61).

[49] *Quaedam sunt tam perspicua, simulque tam simplicia, ut nunquam possimus de iis cogitare, quin vera esse credamus* (AT VII, 145).

freely, since this is of the essence of the will, but none the less infallibly, towards a good clearly known to it'.[50]

The *Principles* repeats and expands the doctrine of the *Meditations*. But when free will is first mentioned in Principle 37 it looks as if Descartes is attributing liberty of indifference to the assent of clear truths. He writes: 'It is a supreme perfection in man to act voluntarily or freely, and thus to be in a special sense the author of his own actions, and to deserve praise for them. . . . It is more to our credit that we embrace the truth when we do, because we do this freely, than it would be if we could not but embrace it.'[51] He goes on to say that in *many* cases 'we have power to assent or not assent at our pleasure'.[52] During the exercise of Cartesian doubt 'we were conscious of freedom to abstain from believing what was not quite certain and thoroughly examined'.[53]

However, this freedom does not hold in all cases, as soon transpires. It does not extend to things which *are* certain and examined: because there were some things which even to a Cartesian doubter were beyond doubt.

The impossibility of withholding assent from clearly perceived truths is explicitly reasserted in Principle 43. This (principle) is imprinted by nature on the minds of all in such a way that as often as we perceive something clearly, we spontaneously assent to it, and we cannot in any way doubt that it is true.[54] Despite a superficial impression, therefore, there is no difference of doctrine between the *Meditations* and the *Principles*.

The *Principles* were published in 1644. On the 2nd of May of the same year, Descartes wrote to the Jesuit Denis Mesland, then

[50] *Rei cogitantis voluntas fertur, voluntarie quidem et libere, hoc enim est de essentia voluntatis, sed nihilominus infallibiliter, in bonum sibi clare cognitum* (AT VII, 166).
[51] *Summa quaedam in homine perfectio est quod agat per voluntatem, hoc est libere, atque ita peculiari quodam modo sit author suarum actionum, et ob ipsas laudem mereatur. . . . Magis profecto nobis tribuendum est, quod verum amplectamur, cum amplectimur, quia voluntarie id agimus, quam si non possemus non amplecti* (AT VIII, 19). At first sight this appears to mean that when we embrace truth clearly seen we are free not to embrace it; but from the sequel it is clear that this is not so. Perhaps Descartes means that in such a case the credit goes not to us but to the author of our nature, as the credit for the precise operation of a machine goes to its maker.
[52] *Multis ad arbitrium vel assentiri vel non assentiri possimus.*
[53] *Hanc in nobis libertatem esse experiebamur, ut possemus ab iis credendis abstinere, quae non plane certa erant et explorata.*
[54] *Ita omnium animis a natura impressum est, ut quoties aliquid clare percipimus, ei sponte assentiamus, et nullo modo possimus dubitare quin sit verum* (AT VIII, 21).

in his final year as a theology undergraduate at La Flèche, a letter which contains his fullest treatment of the problem of free will. The most important part of the letter is a commentary on the passage from the *Meditations* '*ex magna luce in intellectu sequitur magna propensio in voluntate*'. Descartes agrees with Mesland that one can suspend one's judgement; but only by distracting one's attention; one cannot refrain from desiring a good clearly seen to be good. 'If we see very clearly that something is good for us it is very difficult—and on my view impossible, as long as one continues in the same thought—to stop the course of our desire. But the nature of the soul is such that it does not attend for more than a moment to a single thing; and so as soon as our attention turns from the reasons which make us know that a thing is good for us, we can call up before our mind some other reason to make us doubt of it, and so suspend our judgement, or perhaps even make a contrary judgement.'[55] This is in perfect accord with the *Meditations* theory; indeed it is simply an application to the will's function of pursuing the good of a principle explicitly stated in the Fifth Meditation, and more clearly in the Second Replies, about the will's other function of judging the truth. 'I am indeed so constituted that I cannot but believe something to be true at the time of perceiving it clearly and distinctly. But I am likewise so constituted that I cannot fix my mind's eye constantly on the same object so as to perceive it clearly; and the memory of a previous judgement often comes back to me when I am no longer attending to my arguments for having made it. Consequently, other arguments might now be adduced which would readily upset my view if I had no knowledge of God.'[56]

In the *Meditations* Descartes did not explain how the will falls into sin as explicitly as he explained how the will falls into error.

[55] *Voyant très clairement qu'une chose nous est propre, il est très mal aisé, et même, comme je crois, impossible, pendant qu'on demeure en cette pensée, d'arrêter le cours de notre désir. Mais, parce que la nature de l'âme est de n'être quasi qu'un moment attentive à une même chose, sitôt que notre attention se détourne des raisons qui nous font connaître que cette chose nous est propre, et que nous retenons seulement en notre mémoire qu'elle nous a paru désirable, nous pouvons représenter à notre esprit quelque autre raison qui nous en fasse douter, et ainsi suspendre notre jugement, et même aussi peut-être en former un contraire* (AM VI, 144).

[56] *Etsi enim eius sim naturae ut, quamdiu aliquid valde clare et distincte percipio, non possim non credere verum esse, quia tamen eius etiam sum naturae ut non possim obtutum mentis in eandem rem semper defigere ad illam clare percipiendam, recurratque saepe memoria iudicii ante facti, cum non amplius attendo ad rationes propter quas tale quid iudicavi, rationes aliae possunt quae me, si Deum ignorarem, facile ab opinione deiicerent* (AT VII, 69).

This, he told Mesland, was because he wanted to stay within the limits of natural philosophy and not to involve himself in theological controversies. In this private letter, he is willing to be explicit. 'If we saw clearly (that what we are doing is evil) it would be impossible to sin as long as we saw it in that fashion; that is why they say that whoever sins does so in ignorance.'[57] This was no novelty, but something which he had said in private as early as 24 April, 1637. Defending against Mersenne the statement in the *Discourse* that in order to do well it was sufficient to judge well Descartes had adopted a familiar scholastic viewpoint. 'The will does not tend towards evil except in so far as it is presented to it by the intellect under some aspect of goodness—that is why they say that everyone who sins does so in ignorance. So that if the intellect never presented anything to the will as good without its actually being so, the will could never go wrong in its choice. But the intellect often presents different things to the will at the same time.'[58] This passage clearly implies that the will cannot go against the intellect unless the intellect itself is somehow on both sides of the fence at the same time. In such a case, of course, the perception of the intellect would be confused rather than clear and distinct; and so once again we can draw the conclusion that the will cannot resist the clear and distinct perceptions of the intellect.

In the letter to Mesland Descartes ventures so far into theology as to discuss the merits of Christ. 'A man may earn merit, even though, seeing very clearly what he must do, he does it infallibly and without any indifference, as Jesus Christ did during his earthly life.'[59] How is this to be reconciled with the teaching of the *Principles* that we deserve no praise for what we cannot but do? Descartes explains that the praise is for paying attention.

[57] *Si nous le voyions clairement, il nous serait impossible de pécher, pendant le temps que nous le verrions en cetter sorte; c'est pourquoi on dit que omnis peccans est ignorans* (AM VI, 145).
[58] *Voluntas non fertur in malum, nisi quatenus ei sub aliqua ratione boni repraesentatur ab intellectu, d'ou vient ce mot: omnis peccans est ignorans; en sorte que si jamais l'entendement ne représentait rien à la volonté comme bien, qui ne le fut, elle ne pourrait manquer en son élection. Mais il lui représente souvent diverses choses en même temps'* (AT I, 367). Most commentators seem not to have noticed—and perhaps Descartes himself was not aware—that the dictum he here quotes approvingly *'omnis peccans est ignorans'* is a quotation from his adversary Aristotle *(agnoei oun pas ho mochtheros,* N. Eth. III, 1110b28).
[59] *On ne laisse pas de mériter, bien que, voyant très clairement ce qu' il faut faire, on le fasse infailliblement, et sans aucune indifférence, comme a fait Jésus-Christ en cette vie* (AM VI, 145).

'Since a man has the power not always to attend perfectly to what he ought to do, it is a good action to pay attention and thus to ensure that our will follows so promptly the light of our understanding that it is in no way indifferent.'[60] The doctrine then is clear. In the face of clear and distinct perception, freedom to act in a contrary sense is possible only by inattention.

In this letter Descartes makes a comparison between his terminology and that used by the scholastics, especially Jesuit scholastics such as those who taught Mesland. For him, indifference does not mean complete absence of knowledge; but the more the known reasons balance each other out, the more indifference there is. 'You regard freedom as not precisely indifference (in this sense) but rather as a real and positive power to determine oneself; and so the difference between us is a merely verbal one, since I agree that the will has such a power. However, I do not see that it makes any difference to the power whether it is accompanied by indifference, which you agree is an imperfection, or whether it is not so accompanied, when there is nothing in the understanding except light, as in the case of the blessed who are confirmed in grace. And so I call free whatever is voluntary, whereas you wish to restrict the name to the power to determine oneself only if accompanied by indifference. But so far as concerns names, I wish above all to follow usage and precedent.'[61] Indeed, in treating 'voluntary' and 'free' as synonymous, Descartes was following the precedent of Gibieuf's *De Libertate Dei et Creaturae*. But Gibieuf was consciously going against the prevailing scholastic tradition which made a distinction between the two. According to most scholastics, the saints in heaven loved God voluntarily (because they did so willingly and not reluctantly) but not freely (since, clearly seeing the goodness of God, they

---

[60] *Car l'homme pouvant n'avoir pas toujours une parfait attention aux choses qu'il doit faire, c'est une bonne action que de l'avoir, et de faire, par son moyen, que notre volonté suive si fort la lumière de notre entendement qu'elle ne soit point du tout indifférente* (ibid.).

[61] *Ainsi, puisque vous ne mettez pas la liberté dans l'indifférence précisément, mais dans une puissance réelle et positive de se determiner, il n'y a de différence entre nos opinions que pour le nom; car j'avoue que cette puissance est en la volonté. Mais, parce que je ne vois point qu'elle soit autre, quand elle est accompagnée de l'indifférence, laquelle vous avouez être une imperfection, que quand elle n'en est point accompagnée, et qu'il n'y a rien dans l'entendement que de la lumière, comme dans celui des bienheureux qui sont confirmés en grâce, je nomme généralement libre, tout ce qui est volontaire, et vous voulez restreindre ce nom à la puissance de se déterminer, qui est accompagnée de l'indifférence. Mais je ne désire rien tant, touchant les noms, que de suivre l'usage et l'exemple* (AM V, 144).

DESCARTES ON THE WILL

could not do otherwise).[62] On this view, everything free was voluntary, but not everything voluntary was free; and the will, as such, was the capacity for voluntary action, and so not synonymous with the *free* will or *liberum arbitrium*.

Thus far, Descartes' doctrine of liberty is all of a piece. But there remains one crucial document to consider. This is the letter listed by Adam and Milhaud as being written to Mesland on 9 February 1645; it is number 463 in their collection. M. Alquié, in his *La Découverte Metaphysique de l'Homme chez Descartes*,[63] and in the notes to the Garnier edition of Descartes' works, regards this as marking a decisive break in Descartes' thought. Now at last, in this letter, according to Alquié, Descartes admits that one can reject an evident perception at the moment of perceiving it. '*Il est donc possible, selon Descartes, (contrairement à l'avis de presque tous les commentateurs) de nier l'évidence en presence de l'évidence même, de se detourner du bien sous le charme même de son attrait*' (op. cit. 289). Hitherto, it was only by ignorance or inattention that Descartes allowed the possibility of sin or error; in this letter, Alquié believes, Descartes' doctrine '*permet de refuser l'évidence et le bien en connaissance de cause*'. Alquié quotes from the letter: 'It is always open to us to hold back from pursuing a clearly known good or from admitting a clearly perceived truth, provided we consider it a good thing to demonstrate the freedom of our will by so doing.' And he concludes '*Il ne s'agit pas, en la lettre de 9 février, de la faiblesse d'une attention se pouvant malaisement fixer sur un object unique, ni de l'élan qui, dans les Méditations, empêchait la conscience de se limiter à des objects finis et la portait vers l'infinie lui-même par un perpétuel dépassement. Ce qui nous détourne du bien, c'est la mauvaise foi que commande l'égoïsme, et sans dout ce désir d'être Dieu qui, dans la Bible, apparaissait déjà comme la source première du péché. Qu'est en effet ce libre arbitre qu'il s'agit d'attester, sinon précisément nous-mêmes?*'

No one, says Alquié, has tried to expound Descartes' doctrine of freedom in this letter ' *sans essayer d'en affaiblir le tragique*'. I

---

[62] Op. cit., 56. *Voluntati qua natura inest sua libertas*. . . . *Video responderi posse rationem liberi non esse rationem voluntatis, latiusque patere voluntatem quam libertatem: quippe voluntatem ad omne bonum se extendere, libertatem autem ad id tantum quod possit amari vel non amari cum indifferentia* . . . *sed si radix libertatis attente consideretur, facile erit non deprehendere solum sed convincere voluntatem nihil esse nise libertatem.*

[63] 2 ed. (Paris, 1966).

fear I must range myself with the commentators who have been insensitive to the tragedy. I observe first that to base on this letter a theory of an evolution in Descartes' thought is to build on sand. No one knows for certain to whom this letter was written or when. It is given by Clerselier in French as part of a composite letter to Mersenne whose other parts date from 1630 and 1637; but as it alludes to the *Meditations* it must be later than 1640. Adam and Tannery printed it in their third volume in French as a letter to Mersenne with the hypothetical date of May 1641. Alquié says that at this date the letter '*serait incompréhensible, les affirmations qu'elle contient ne pouvant se situer qu'au terme d'une évolution de pensée comprenant elle-même les Principes et la lettre de 2 mai 1644, contemporaine de leur impression*'. But as the only evidence for this evolution is Alquié's interpretation of this very letter, the progress of the evolution cannot be used to date it. Adam and Tannery later found a Latin text of the letter in a MS of the Bibliothèque Mazarine which gave it as a continuation of the letter in French to Mesland of 9 February 1645; accordingly they inserted it in their fifth volume after this letter, and it is retained in this place by Adam and Milhaud in their collection. On internal evidence there seems little doubt that this Latin text is more likely to be the original than the French text given by Clerselier;[64] but the attachment to the letter to Mesland is very dubious. All Descartes' letters to Mesland, as almost always to French-speaking correspondents, are in French, not in Latin. If this fragment belongs to the letter of 9 February, we have a change of language in the middle: why should a letter begun in French end in Latin? Moreover, there is no allusion to the previous letter on free will to Mesland, though some of the same points are covered. It seems most likely that the compiler of the Bibliothéque Mazarine collection put together letters on transubstantiation and liberty, most but not all of which were to Mesland, rather in the way that Clerselier put together the composite letter to Mersenne from various draft documents he found among Descartes' papers. We must resign ourselves to the fact that we know neither the date nor the destination of this letter.

Whatever the date of the letter, there is in fact no contradic-

[64] A note in the Institut copy of Clerselier mentions both that the original of the fragment given by Clerselier is in Latin, and that the date and destination must be considered unknown (AT III, 378).

tion between its teaching and that of the earlier letter to Mesland. The passage on which M. Alquié builds his theory can easily be explained in accordance with Descartes' regular doctrine; and there are other passages which flatly contradict the interpretation put on the letter by Alquié. The letter is so short and so important that I propose at this point to insert a translation of the whole of it.

Descartes (to Mesland) 9 February 1645

As for the freedom of the will, I entirely agree with what the Reverend Father here wrote. Let me explain my opinion more fully. I would like you to notice that 'indifference' seems to me to mean here the state of the will when it is not impelled one way rather than another by any perception of truth or goodness. This was the sense in which I took it when I said that the lowest degree of liberty was that by which we determine ourselves to things to which we are indifferent. But perhaps others mean by 'indifference' a positive faculty of determining oneself to one or other of two contraries, that is to say to pursue or avoid, to affirm or deny. I do not deny that the will has this positive faculty. Indeed, I think it has it not only with respect to those actions to which it is not pushed by any evident reasons on one side rather than on the other, but also with respect to all other actions; so that when a very evident reason moves us in one direction, although, morally speaking, we can hardly move in the contrary direction, absolutely we can. For it is always open to us to hold back from pursuing a clearly known good, or from admitting a clearly perceived truth, provided we consider it a good thing to demonstrate the freedom of our will by so doing.

It must be noted also that liberty can be considered in the actions of the will before they are elicited, or after they are elicited.

Considered with respect to the time before they are elicited, it entails indifference in the second sense but not in the first. Although, when we contrast our own judgement with the commandments of others we say that we are freer to do those things which have not been prescribed to us by others and in which we are allowed to follow our own judgement, we cannot similarly make a contrast within the field of our own judgements and thought and say that we are freer to do those things which seem neither good nor evil, or in which there are many reasons pro but as many reasons contra, than in those in which we see much more good than evil. For a greater liberty consists either in a greater facility in determining oneself, or of a greater use of the positive power which we have of following the worse although we see the better. If we follow the course which appears to have the most reasons in its favour, we determine ourselves more easily; if we follow the opposite, we make more use of that positive power; and thus we can always act more freely in those cases in which we see much more good than evil than in those cases which are called *adiaphora* or indifferent. In this sense too the things which are commanded us by others, and which we would not otherwise do spontaneously, we do less freely than the things which are not commanded; because the judgement that these things are difficult to do is opposed to the judgement that it is good to do what is commanded; and the more equally these two judgements move us the more indifference, in the first sense, they confer on us.

But liberty considered in the acts of the will at the moment when they are elicited does not entail any indifference either in the first or second sense; because what is done cannot remain undone once it is being done. But it consists simply in ease of operation; and at that point freedom, spontaneity and voluntariness are the same thing. It was in this sense that I wrote that I took a course more freely the more reasons drove me towards it; because it is certain that in that case our will moves itself with greater facility and force.

In the first part of this letter Descartes makes explicit a distinction between two senses of 'indifferent' which was implicit in his 1644 letter when he said that indifference did not imply ignorance, and that wherever there was occasion for sin there was ignorance. When he said that, Descartes clearly did not mean that there could only be sin where the reasons for acting were equally balanced on either side; consequently, he must have meant that there was an indifference which consisted in the possibility of acting against the weight of reason. It is this ability—which we might nickname 'the liberty of perversion'[65]—which Descartes now explicitly distinguishes from indifference in the sense of a balance of reasons. Adding this distinction to the distinction

[65] *Potestas . . . sequendi deteriora, quamvis meliora videamus* (AM VI, 198).

between two kinds of liberty which we saw in the 1644 letter, we get the following table.

$$\text{Liberty} = \text{Voluntas} \begin{cases} \text{Liberty of spontaneity} \\ \text{Liberty of indifference} \begin{cases} \text{Perversion} \\ \text{Balance} \end{cases} \end{cases}$$

So far the two letters are perfectly compatible. According to Alquié, the two letters differ crucially because according to the 1644 letter we do not enjoy liberty of perversion while we have a clear perception of good whereas in letter number 463 we do so. However, it is perfectly possible to reconcile the two. When Descartes says in letter 463 that it is always open to us to hold back from pursuing a clearly known good, or from admitting a clearly perceived truth, he need not mean that we can do this at the very moment of perceiving the good and the true. Rather, we must distract our attention, as he said in the 1644 letter. One way of doing this would be to dwell on the thought that it would be a good thing to demonstrate our free will by perversity. This would provide a reason in the contrary sense, without which the will could not act; and *eo ipso* this would render the perception of truth and goodness unclear; we would, as he said in the 1644 letter, 'merely see confusedly that what we are doing is bad, or remember that we judged it so in the past'. In the 1644 letter he says that we can suspend our judgement 'by representing to our mind some reason to make us doubt of the truth'; letter number 463 suggests a reason one could use.[66]

Alquié sees the possibility of such an interpretation, but says that it would satisfy a merely conceptual demand and would ignore the conflict of our life. But it is possible that Descartes shared a concern for merely conceptual demands; and after all, this is not a minor point in his system. To abandon the theory that clear and distinct perception necessitates the will is to call in question the whole validation of reason in which the *Meditations* culminates. The mark of a clear and distinct idea is that it is one which however much we may exercise our free will we cannot doubt; the only way to find truth is to stick to clear and distinct

---

[66] Without some such reason, doubt would be impossible, as Descartes explained to Gassendi (AT X, 205).

ideas; the only way to find out which ideas are clear and distinct is to do our damnedest to doubt them and fail to do so. But if clear and distinct ideas can be doubted at the moment they are intuited, we should never have genuine and certain knowledge of anything, we would be back in the morass of doubts of the First Meditation.

The interpretation I have suggested is confirmed by the passage of the letter which immediately follows that on which Alquié rests his case. Descartes distinguishes liberty before the will's act, and liberty during the act. This suggests that we must make a further distinction in the chart we drew, a distinction between simultaneous and subsequent perversion. Thus we have

$$\begin{matrix} \text{Liberty} \\ = \\ \text{Voluntas} \end{matrix} \begin{cases} \text{Spontaneity} \\ \text{Indifference} \end{cases} \begin{cases} \text{Perversion} \\ \text{Balance} \end{cases} \begin{cases} \text{Subsequent} \\ \text{Simultaneous} \end{cases}$$

Combining together the data of the two letters, we get the following results. The Blessed in heaven and Christ on earth enjoy liberty of spontaneity, but no liberty of indifference, of any kind, not even the liberty of subsequent perversion. An ordinary man with a clear and distinct idea of what is true and what is good enjoys liberty of spontaneity and liberty of subsequent perversion, but not liberty of simultaneous perversion nor indifference in the sense of balance. An ordinary man with a confused idea of what is true and good enjoys liberty of simultaneous perversion, but only a man who sees no reason to one side rather than another enjoys the full indifference. Such a man, Descartes says, does not enjoy the liberty of spontaneity enjoyed by the others.[67] His argument for this will be considered in a moment.

The final paragraph of the letter 463 is reminiscent of an argument which occurs in Gibieuf's *De Libertate Dei* against the Jesuits who define liberty in terms of an absolute indifference to act or not to act.[68] If that is what liberty consists in, Gibieuf

[67]	Blessed	C & D	Prob.	Balance
Liberty of Spontaneity	Yes	Yes	Yes	No (Yes)
Liberty of Subs. Perversion	No	Yes	Yes	Yes (No)
Liberty of Simul. Perversion	No	No	Yes	Yes (No)
Liberty of Balance	No	No	No	Yes

[68] This is one of several indications that the Reverend Father mentioned at the beginning of the letter is, as Baillet said, Gibieuf. Another is that the definition of indifference Descartes attributes to the Reverend Father is the one

argued, then a man never acts less freely than when he acts freely. For when a man acts, he is not indifferent with regard to acting, but is determined by his very act. To say that it is enough that he could not act when he was on the point of acting, Gibieuf argued, is to say that liberty is only for future acts *qua* future. On Gibieuf's own view, a man was free if he acted for the sake of the supreme good; and this could be true of him while he was actually acting.[69]

I think that the argument of Gibieuf and Descartes is confused, though it is not easy to explain just where it goes wrong. I do not think, as I once did, that it depends simply on a fallacious inference of modal logic from

> It is not possible that both *p* and not *p*

to If *p*, then it is not possible that not *p*.

In addition to modality, the argument involves subtle points about tense and action which it would take us too far round to investigate. But the paragraph does contain a point which tells against Alquié. Once one acts, Descartes says, the notions of liberty and spontaneity collapse into each other. This would be altogether untrue on Alquié's view, because in the case of someone with a clear and distinct idea acting with simultaneous perversity, there would be free action, but not spontaneous action; since the man would not be acting with that preponderance of reasons on his side which makes the operation easy and constitutes spontaneity.

Finally I wish to consider the penultimate paragraph of the letter. There is something very dubious about Descartes' argument here to show that indifference of balance is the lowest degree of liberty. He argues that a man enjoys least liberty when the reasons are balanced, because he then enjoys less liberty of spontaneity than when he acts in accord with the greater array of reasons, and less liberty of perversity than when he acts in accord

---

Gibieuf uses, and not the Jesuit one which Mesland accepted and Gibieuf attacked. This suggests that Adam and Tannery's first thoughts on the dating of the letter were perhaps better than their second, since it was in the 30s that we know Descartes was interested in Gibieuf's book.

[69] *Quarta probatio ducitur ex contradictione aperta quam includit natura libertatis, ut eam exponere consueverent per indifferentiam absolutam ad agendum et non agendum. Si enim ea sit conditio libertatis, homo nunquam minus libere agit quam cum libere agit. Qui enim agit, non est indifferens ad agendum, sed determinatur actu suo* (op. cit. 13; cf. also 165).

with the lesser array of reasons. He could just as well have argued that a man was most at liberty when the reasons were balanced, since he then enjoys more liberty of perversity than when the majority of reasons are on his side, and more liberty of spontaneity than when the majority of reasons are against him. In fact, having once distinguished liberty of spontaneity from liberty of perversity, Descartes should have said that in the one sense of liberty, action in indifferent matters was freer than action upon clear reasons, and in another sense it was less free. But then he could not have said, what he also wanted to say, that there was a single scale of freedom on which the liberty of indifference occupied the lowest place. This shows that Descartes' theory of freedom will not do as a philosophical account; but it is an incoherence which was present in the theory from the beginning. The doctrine of the *Meditations*, the *Principles* and the letters is all of a piece. I see no reason for thinking that at the age of forty-nine Descartes underwent a spectacular conversion from rationalism to existentialism.

CARTESIAN PRIVACY

It is frequently said that one of the achievements of Wittgenstein was to provide a refutation of Cartesian dualism. In this paper I wish to examine such a claim in detail.

Descartes, by making epistemology the centre of philosophical inquiry, created a new philosophy of mind. The novelty of this philosophy lay less in its explicit theses than in the whole perspective in which it viewed the relationship between the mental and the physical. Still, Descartes' epistemological and psychological innovations are well summed up in his own dictum that mind is better known than body.

This thesis was novel in two ways.

First, medieval Aristotelians had taught that the human mind, as we know it, was most at home in the study of the nature of physical bodies. Intellect is a capacity, so their theory ran, and capacities are known through their exercise. But the proper exercise of the human intellect as we know it is the investigation of the physical universe. Knowledge of the human mind, therefore, must be secondary to, almost parasitic on, knowledge of the external world. For we can know about the human capacity to know only if we can see that capacity at work; and that capacity is best seen at work within the field which is its proper study (cf. Aquinas, *Summa Theologica*, Ia 87, 1c).

Secondly, the boundaries between mind and body were redrawn by Descartes. Mind, for him, is *res cogitans*, and *cogitatio* includes not only intellectual meditation but also volition, emotion, pain, pleasure, mental images, and sensations. For Aquinas, by contrast, the boundary between spirit and nature was not between consciousness and clockwork, it was between intellect and sense. It was understanding and judging and willing, not feeling aches or seeing colours or having mental images, which for him set mind apart from matter. The former were possible without a body. God and the angels understand and will and judge no less than men. The latter were inconceivable without a living organism: disembodied spirits neither see nor hear, feel neither joy nor sorrow, have neither imagination nor memory images (*Summa Theologica*, Ia 77, 8). The difference between the two comes out clearly in the case of pain. For Descartes, pain, in the strictest sense, is something spiritual: however much the incautious may confuse the pure sensation of pain with an erroneous judgement about its physical causes, none the less a *res cogitans* can feel pain though he has no body at all. For Aquinas, pain, in the strictest sense, is something physical; the disembodied spirits in hell suffer because of the thwarting of their wills, not through aches or pains (*Summa Theologica*, Ia 64, 3; cited by Geach, *Mental Acts*, 116).

Descartes' innovations influenced philosophers outside the Cartesian tradition. Ideas, impressions, and sense-data are all, by Cartesian standards, mental entities; and for the British empiricists they are all epistemologically prior to the physical substances of the problematic external world. For Locke, Berkeley and Hume, no less than for Descartes, mind is better known than body in the sense that the internal is more certain than the external, the private is prior to the public. The philosophical viability of the Cartesian notion of mind concerns not only the historian of Descartes but anyone interested in epistemology and philosophical psychology. But I propose to approach the question by a study of the text of Descartes. What does Descartes mean by *res cogitans*?

'*Cogitare*' and '*penser*' are naturally translated 'think'. Descartes, as has been noted, uses the verbs to record many experiences which we would not naturally describe as thoughts. It has been said that the words in the current French and Latin of Descartes' time had a sense wider than that of the modern English equivalent with its predominantly intellectual reference. This may be so. However, French and Latin usage was never as wide as that to be found in Descartes: at no time was it natural to call a headache or a feeling of hunger a *cogitatio* or *pensée*. Moreover, the English use of 'thought' is not purely intellectualistic: when a young man's fancy turns to thoughts of love, the thoughts include emotions, desires, and intentions. In fact, it seems that

Descartes was consciously extending the use of the words '*cogitare*' and '*penser*'. This is brought out by the misunderstandings of his contemporaries. Thus Mersenne objected that if the nature of man consisted solely of thought, then man has no will. 'I do not see that this follows,' Descartes had to explain, 'for willing, understanding, imagining and feeling are simply different ways of thinking, which all belong to the soul' (to Mersenne, 27. 4. 1637, *AT* I, 366). To another correspondent, a year later, he wrote: 'There is nothing entirely in our power except our thoughts; at least if you take the word "thought" as I do, for all the operations of the soul, in such a way that not only meditations and acts of the will, but even the functions of sight and hearing, and the resolving on one movement rather than another, in so far as they depend on the soul, are all thoughts' (*AT* II, 36). I shall use the traditional translation 'thought' for '*cogitatio*' and '*pensée*'. The English word will seem unnatural in some contexts, but no more unnatural than the corresponding words seemed in similar contexts to Descartes' contemporaries.

Descartes extended the concept of *thought* because of a feature which he believed to attach to all the operations of the soul. 'By the noun *thought*,' he wrote in the *Principles*, 'I understand everything which takes place in us so that we are conscious of it (*nobis consciis*), in so far as it is an object of awareness' (*AT* VIII, 7). When he was setting out his terms *more geometrico* in answer to the Second Objections, he gave a similar definition, adding that the consciousness must be immediate. 'Under the term 'thought' I include everything which is in us in such a way that we are immediately conscious of it . . . I added 'immediately' for the purpose of excluding the consequences of thoughts; voluntary movements, for instance, depend upon thoughts but are not themselves thoughts' (*AT* VII, 161).

What is common, then, to all the operations of the mind is consciousness. Consciousness carries with it indubitability, and this is what makes the '*cogito ergo sum*' suitable as a first principle. '*Sum*' is the first indubitable existential judgement; and it is indubitable because the premise on which it is based, '*cogito*,' is indubitable. In the *Discourse on Method*, the mental activity referred to by '*je pense*' is the attempt to think everything false; in the *Meditations* the *cogitatio* in question is the thought of Descartes' own existence. But any conscious activity is capable of providing a premise for the *cogito*, as Descartes explains in the *Principles*. 'There is nothing that gives rise to knowledge of any object which does not even more certainly lead us to know our thought. For instance, if I persuade myself that there is an earth because I touch or see it, by that very fact, and for much better reason, I should be persuaded that my thought exists, because it may be that I think I touch the earth even though there is possibly no earth in existence at all, but it is not possible that I—that is my soul—should be non-existent while it has this thought. We can draw the same conclusion from all the other things which come into our thought: namely that we who think them exist' (*AT* VIII, 8).

Sensation, then, as well as intellectual thought, is a thought capable of founding the certainty of one's own existence. But does not sensation presuppose a body, as Descartes himself says in the Second Meditation (*AT* VII, 27): how then can its occurrence be certain while the existence of body is doubtful? Descartes explains that there are two different ways of taking 'sensation'. 'Suppose I say I see (or I am walking) therefore I exist. If I take this to refer to vision (or walking) as a corporeal action, the conclusion is not absolutely certain; for as often happens during sleep, I may think I am seeing though I do not open my eyes (or think I am walking although I do not change my place); and it may even be that I have no body. But if I take it to refer to the actual sensation or awareness (*conscientia*) of seeing (or walking) then it is quite certain; for in that case it has regard to the mind, and it is the mind alone that has a sense or experience of itself seeing (or walking).' Sensation so understood, he says, is thought (*AT* VIII, 7).

In making this identification Descartes is not so much extending the sense of *cogitatio* as altering that of *sensus*. If Macbeth says he sees a dagger where no dagger is, we may hesitate to say whether he *sees* anything at all; but it is perfectly natural to say he *thinks* he sees a dagger. Now this same thought, on Descartes' view, occurs also when Macbeth really is, in the normal sense, seeing a dagger; and it is thought of this kind in which sensation strictly so called consists and which provides a premise for the *cogito*. Such thoughts can be mistaken, but their existence cannot be doubted. 'It is I who have sensations, or who perceive corporeal objects as it were by the senses. Thus, I am now seeing

CARTESIAN PRIVACY 117

light, hearing a noise, feeling heat. These objects are unreal, for I am asleep; but at least I seem to see, to hear, to be warmed. This cannot be unreal; and this is what is properly called my sensation; further, sensation, precisely so regarded, is nothing but an act of thought' (Second Meditation, *AT* VII, 29).

In this theory of Descartes there is an unnaturalness and an ambiguity.

The unnaturalness is this. Comparison of the various texts of Descartes make clear that what is referred to by 'think' in 'thinking I am seeing' and by 'seem' in 'seeming to hear' is to be identified with the consciousness or perception by which Descartes defines the nature of *cogitatio* or thought. (In the passage from the *Principles*, for instance, '*putare me videre*' is used in parallel with '*conscientia videndi*' and with '*mens cogitat se videre*'.) But we cannot say that the consciousness, or perception, or awareness of sensation may occur whether or not sensation occurs; 'to be conscious of', 'to perceive' and 'to be aware of' are all success-verbs, so that one can only be conscious of, perceive, and be aware of what is really the case. On the other hand, it is odd to say that 'seeming to see' or 'thinking that one sees' may occur whether or not seeing occurs; 'seeming to see' and 'thinking that one sees' seem to be phrases designed to cover just the case in which one *doesn't* see. The *cogitatio* of seeing is meant to be what is common to the genuine case and the doubtful case. Perhaps it is no accident that there is no natural way of referring to such a common element.

The ambiguity is this. Sometimes, consciousness appears to be something which accompanies thought (as in the *Second Replies*, quoted above); sometimes it appears to be something which is identical with thought (as in the passage quoted above from the *Second Meditation*). The ambiguity is multiplied in the two versions of Descartes' reply to Hobbes (*AT* VII, 176; IX, 137). The Latin version tells us that there are some acts which are called cogitative, such as understanding, willing, imagining, sensing; 'these all fall under the common concept of thought, perception or consciousness (*qui omni sub ratione communi cogitationis, sive perceptionis, sive conscientiae conveniunt*)'. The authorized French version has: 'these all have in common that they cannot occur without thought, or perception, or consciousness and awareness (*tous lesquels conviennent entre eux en ce qu'ils ne peuvent être sans pensée, ou perception, ou conscience et connaissance)'*. Both versions here identify thought and consciousness; but the Latin regards particular mental acts as species of thought-consciousness, whereas the French regards them as accompanied by thought-consciousness. We shall later see reason to believe that this ambiguity is not an accidental defect in Descartes' terminology, but is the consequence of an essential element in his system. For the moment it suffices to note that the ambiguity arises naturally from the way in which *cogitatio* is introduced. Sensation is a conscious act in the sense of being itself a mode of consciousness—to see a circle and to feel a circle are two different ways of being conscious of the circle. But willing is not a conscious act in the same way: to want to be certain is not to be conscious of being certain; wanting is a conscious act in the different sense that if I want something, I am conscious that I want it. Equally, it might be said, if I perceive something, then I am conscious that I perceive it. But even so, there is the possibility of ambiguity. Willing is conscious in the sense of being an object of consciousness; sensation is conscious not only in this sense but also in the sense of being a mode of consciousness.

The issue is further complicated because what we do voluntarily we are normally conscious of doing. Thus, Descartes told the Marquis of Newcastle that there are some of our actions which are not managed by our thought 'for it often happens that we walk and that we eat without thinking in any way of what we are doing; likewise, without using our reason, we push away things that are harmful and parry blows which are aimed at us; and even if we expressly wished not to put our hands in front of our head when we fall, we could not stop ourselves' (*AT* IV, 573). Here Descartes seems to treat as equivalent *attending to* an action and *intending* an action; we put up our hands involuntarily but not inadvertently; we eat our food without attention but not without intention. The analogy between sensation and action seems to be merely this: just as I can think I am seeing without seeing, so I can think I am breathing without breathing (*AT* II, 37). As in perception, so in action there is *thought*, in this sense. But it is not clear what is the relation of this thought to volition.

It would be wrong to identify the thought that I am seeing or the thought that I am walking with the belief that I am seeing or walking in the ordinary sense of 'see' and 'walk'. The occurrence of such a belief is not a necessary condition for the occurrence of the corresponding thought: Descartes, during his period of doubt, has the thought that he is seeing a light—that is, it seems to him that he is seeing a light—but he refrains from believing this. Again, the occurrence of such a belief is not a sufficient condition for the occurrence of the corresponding thought. The intellectual perception of the injury of a limb is not the same as the feeling of pain in that limb (*AT* VII, 82), and presumably a man whose limbs were anaesthetized and knew that he was moving them only because he was told so would not have the *cogitatio* of moving his limbs. Rather, to have the thought that p is to have an experience similar to the experience I have when we would normally say that p is the case. Does the experience have to be so similar as to be indistinguishable, or merely so similar as to be *de facto* not distinguished? This is a question to which we shall have to return.

Two things emerge from the consideration of *cogitatio* in spite of the questions about its nature which we have left, for the moment, unanswered. First, the relation of thought to its bodily causes and expressions is completely contingent. All our thoughts could be just as they are even if no body ever existed: only the veracity of God assures us that this is not in fact the case. Secondly, the occurrence of thoughts themselves is not open to doubt or error. Thoughts cannot occur without our knowing that they occur; and we cannot think that a thought is occurring unless that thought actually is occurring. The first we are told expressly; the second is presupposed by the structure of the *cogito*. Perhaps I only think I see; but that I think I see cannot be doubted. Note that it is not just the occurrence of *thought* that cannot be doubted, but the occurrence of the particular thought in question (*AT* VII, 29).

We are now in a position to see the precise nature of Descartes' innovation in philosophy of mind. The introduction of *cogitatio* as the defining characteristic of mind is tantamount to the substitution of privacy for rationality as the mark of the mental. For somebody like Aquinas, human beings were distinguished from animals by such things as their capacity to understand geometry and to desire riches. Neither the understanding of geometry nor the desire for riches is a specially private state concerning which the subject is in a position of special authority. I may

I

doubt whether I understand the proof of a particular theorem, and a teacher may be able to show me that I was mistaken about one I believed I understood. I may wonder whether I am adopting a certain policy out of cupidity; and a perceptive friend may be able to settle the question better than I can myself. On such topics my sincere statement is not the last possible word.

On the other hand, if I want to know what sensations somebody is having, what he seems to see or hear, what he is imagining or saying to himself, then I have to give his utterances on the topic a special status. What he says need not be true—he may be insincere, or misunderstand the words he is using—but it cannot be erroneous. Experiences of this kind have the property of indubitability which Descartes ascribes to thought. They are private to their owner in the sense that while others can doubt them, he cannot.

It is clear that privacy, in the sense indicated, is something independent of the rationality discussed above. The discovery of Pythagoras' theorem was a clearly rational activity, and to know this we do not need to know whether Pythagoras worked out the theorem first aloud or in his head. The production of random grunts is not something which calls for rationality, whether I produce them aloud, or in imagination, grunting, as it were, in my mind's throat.

We can now see in what way Wittgenstein's philosophy is relevant to Cartesian dualism. If Descartes' innovation was to identify the mental with the private, Wittgenstein's contribution was to separate the two. Since Wittgenstein, we tend to equate the mental with what is peculiar to language-users; and if Wittgenstein's arguments are valid, languages cannot be private. The *cogito* and the private language argument each lie at the heart of the epistemology and philosophy of mind of their inventors. The *cogito* led to the conclusion that mind is better known than body. The private language argument leads, we might say, to the conclusion that body is better known than mind.

I shall examine Wittgenstein's arguments against private language and try to show in detail how they connect with the Cartesian theses. I shall argue that the referents of the words of Wittgenstein's private language correspond to Descartes' *cogitationes*; and that the properties of these entities from which Wittgenstein sought to show the impossibility of a private language are properties from which an argument could also be drawn against Descartes' system of clear and distinct ideas. The comparison of the two arguments is facilitated by the fact that Wittgenstein took the same example, pain, to illustrate his thesis as Descartes had taken to explain the notion of clear and distinct ideas (*Principles of Philosophy*, I, 46f., 67 ff.).

Descartes did not much reflect on the nature of language. When he uttered the words *cogito ergo sum*, he took it for granted that he knew what they meant. Perhaps, as the Sixth Objections said, he should not have done so; perhaps, in accordance with his methodic doubt he should have questioned whether they meant what he thought they meant. Descartes replied that it was enough to know what thought and existence were 'by that internal cognition which always precedes reflective knowledge and which, when the object is thought and existence, is innate in all men' (*AT* VII, 422). In the *Principles* he explained that when he called the *cogito* the first principle, 'I was not denying that we must first know what is meant by thought, existence, certainty; again, we must know such things as that it is impossible for that which is thinking to be non-existent; but I thought it needless to enumerate these notions, for they are of the greatest simplicity, and by themselves they can give us no knowledge that anything exists' (*AT* VIII, 8).

Still, it seems clear that if a Cartesian *res cogitans* uses a language it must be a private language in the sense defined by Wittgenstein (*Philosophical Investigations*, I, secs. 246, 253). If the language contains words for sensations, then the connection between the words and the sensations must be set up without the intermediary of the natural expression of sensation in bodily behaviour; for the words of the language are supposed to have meaning at a stage at which it is doubtful whether there are any bodies at all.

The word 'pain' in such a language must refer to what Wittgenstein calls 'an immediate private sensation', something which can be known only to the person speaking. For Descartes pain, in the ordinary sense of the word, was something very like perception; whereas taste, say, was a perception of the outer senses, pain was a perception of the inner senses. In this sense, it was subject to deception like the other senses. Thus, in the Sixth Meditation we are told: '[I found error] not only in [judgements] founded on the external senses, but even in those founded on the internal as well; for is there anything more intimate or internal than pain? And yet I have learned from some persons whose arms or legs have been cut off, that they sometimes seemed to feel pain in the part which had been amputated, which made me think that I could not be quite certain that it was a certain member which pained me, even though I felt pain in it' (*AT* VII, 71). In pain, as in sight, we must distinguish what is strictly *cogitatio*. The indubitable *cogitatio* will be the 'immediate private sensation'.

In sections 246 and 253 Wittgenstein explains in what sense 'private' is to be taken. Pain, in the ordinary sense of the word is private in the sense that it is senseless to say of myself that I doubt whether I am in pain and in the sense that one criterion of identity for pains is the identity of their possessor. 'Pain' in the private language is meant to refer to something private in a special sense: a sensation whose existence I can know with certainty and other people cannot.

Now Descartes' *cogitatio* of pain will be private in just this sense. First, it cannot be known with certainty to other people. No bodily manifestation of pain is a sufficient proof of its occurrence; notoriously, Descartes believed that animals displayed all the bodily manifestations of pain without feeling pain itself. Explaining this to the Marquis of Newcastle, Descartes wrote: 'There is not one of our exterior actions, which can assure those who examine them that our body is not just a self-moving machine, but also contains a soul which has thoughts, with the exception of the words or other signs deliberately produced in connection with subjects which occur, without having reference to any passion' (*AT* IV, 574). No bodily behaviour therefore can establish the occurrence of the thought which is pain; even the utterance 'I am in pain', would 'have reference to a passion', and so be disqualified (*AT* IV, 573). Secondly, pain, like any other thought, is known with certainty to the sufferer: pain is clearly and distinctly perceived when it is considered merely as a sensation or thought (*Principles*, I, LXVIII. *AT* VIII, 33).

Wittgenstein objects to the expression 'I know I am in pain'. He wishes to reserve the use of 'know' to cases where deception and doubt are possible, but in fact excluded. In the case of one's own pain the expression of doubt is senseless, so the expression of knowledge rules out nothing. 'It can't be said of me at all (except perhaps as a joke) that I *know* I am in pain. What is it supposed to mean—except perhaps that I *am* in pain?' (*PI*, I, sec. 246).

Here we must return to an ambiguity in Descartes' concept of thought which we left unresolved. Was *cogitatio* identical with *conscientia*, we asked, or was it distinct? If it is identical, then Descartes agrees with Wittgenstein that 'I know I am in pain' means nothing more nor less than 'I am in pain'. Wittgenstein argues in effect that the believer in private sensations must make it both possible and impossible for a sufferer to be mistaken about his pain: possible, if the assertion 'I know I am in pain' is to have any content; impossible, if it is to be universally true (*PI*, I, secs. 246, 258, 270).

Descartes' doctrine of pain seems to be open to a very similar objection. He writes thus, to illustrate the doctrine of clear and distinct ideas. 'The knowledge upon which a certain and incontrovertible judgement can be formed, should not alone be clear but also distinct. I term that clear which is present and apparent to an attentive mind, in the same way as we assert that we see objects clearly when, being present to the regarding eye, they operate upon it with sufficient strength. But the distinct is that which is so precise and different from all other objects that it contains within itself nothing but what is clear. When, for instance, a severe pain is felt, the perception of this pain may be very clear, and yet for all that not distinct, because it is usually confused by the sufferers with the obscure judgement that they form upon its nature, assuming as they do that something exists in the part affected, similar to the sensation of pain of which they are alone clearly conscious' (*Principles*, I, 45–46. *AT* VIII, 22). We are told, however, that we may have a clear knowledge of our sensations 'if we take care to include in the judgements we form of them that only which we know to be precisely contained in our perception of them, and of which we are intimately conscious' (66). Thus 'there is no reason that we should be obliged to believe that the pain, for example, which we feel in our foot, is anything beyond our mind which exists in our foot' (67). We can avoid error if we judge that there is something, of whose nature we are ignorant, which causes the sensation of pain in our minds (cf. the parallel remarks about colour in 70) (*AT* VIII, 32–33).

Now there seem here to be three separate elements in Descartes' account, namely, the pain, the perception of the pain, and the judgement about the pain. The perception of the pain seems to be something distinct from the pain, for there are properties such as clarity and distinctness which belong to the perception but not to the pain. The perception seems to be something distinct from the judgement; judgement is an act of the will which it is in our power to make or withhold, and we are enjoined to restrict our judgement to what we clearly and distinctly perceive. But it is not at all easy to work out what Descartes considers to be the relationships between these three.

In so far as pain is a *cogitatio*, it would seem that pain cannot occur without being perceived. Can it, however, occur without being perceived clearly? Descartes seems to give two different answers to this. On the one hand, he says 'when a man feels great pain, he has a very clear perception of pain' (AT VIII, 22); on the other hand he says that we have a clear perception of our sensations only if we carefully restrict our judgement about them, and this is a condition most difficult to observe. If we ask, however, whether a pain may be perceived clearly without being perceived distinctly, the answer is plain. 'A perception may be clear without being distinct, though not distinct without being clear' (AT VIII, 22). Again, Descartes seems explicit enough on the relationship between perception and judgement. Judgement differs from perception in being an act of the will, in being concerned with extramental reality, and in being liable to error. The faculty of perceiving is infallible, that of assenting can err (AT VIII, 21). Judgement may occur without perception; that is precisely the cause of error: 'people form judgements about what they do not perceive and thus fall into error' (AT VIII, 21). What of the converse case: can clear and distinct perception occur without judgement? Here there are some puzzles. On the one hand we learn that 'we are by nature so disposed to give our assent to things that we clearly perceive, that we cannot possibly doubt of their truth' (AT VIII, 21). Yet on the other hand does not the whole procedure of methodic doubt suppose that one can withhold one's judgement even about what seems most clear?

When we examine Descartes' doctrines closely, the reason for the inconsistencies seems to be this. The clear and distinct perception of pain is not in fact identifiable separately from the occurrence of pain and the judgement about the origin of the pain.

First, to perceive a pain clearly, simply is to have a severe pain. Descartes says: 'I call clear that which is present and manifest to an attentive mind; just as we are said to see clearly objects when they are present and operate strongly, and when our eyes are in the right disposition to survey them' (*AT* VIII, 22). Here there seem to be two elements in clarity: that the object of perception be manifest, and that the perceiving faculty be attentive. In the case of sight, such a distinction is possible; in the case of pain it is illusory. Descartes nowhere suggests what would be the difference between the unclear perception of a manifest pain, and the clear perception of an obscure pain. Yet it must be possible to make out such a difference if the distinction between the occurrence of a pain and the perception of a pain is to be a genuine one.

Secondly, to perceive a pain distinctly is simply to make the correct judgement about one's pain. It is to make the correct, cautious, judgement, 'What I feel is caused by I know not what', rather than the incorrect judgement, 'What I feel is something in my foot'. The difference between a distinct and a confused perception is explained precisely in terms of the nature of the accompanying judgement. When the perception of pain is not distinct, that is because it is 'confused by the sufferers with the obscure judgement that they form upon its nature'.

The perception of pain, then, is not a genuine intermediary between the occurrence of pain and the judgement on pain. Of the two properties of the perception, one, clarity, is really a property of the pain which occurs, and the other, distinctness, is really a property of the judgement made about it. (Cf. *Zettel*, 496).

The criticism which I have just made of the Cartesian notion of the perception of pain is parallel to that which Wittgenstein makes of the notion of 'identifying one's sensations' in the *Philosophical Investigations*. Wittgenstein argues that the expression of doubt has no place in the language-game with 'pain'; the utterance, 'I doubt whether I have a pain', is senseless. But if we cut out the human behaviour which is the expression of pain, then the doubt becomes permissible, since I need a criterion of identity for the sensation, and it is possible that I might identify the sensation wrongly (*PI*, I, sec. 288). The identification of the sensation as pain thus becomes an intermediate step between the occurrence of the pain and the expression of it in the words 'I am in pain'. But in fact there is no room for such an intermediate step. We must either in effect identify recognizing a sensation with having a sensation (so that 'I know I am in pain' means 'I am in pain') or else identify the recognition of the sensation with its expression. This last possibility is explored at 270. 'I discover that whenever I have a particular sensation a manometer shows that my blood pressure rises. So I shall be able to say that my blood pressure is rising without using any apparatus. This is a useful result. And now it seems quite indifferent whether I have recognized the sensation *right* or not. Let us suppose I regularly identify it wrong, it does not matter in the least.' There are in fact only two possibilities of discrepancy between pain and its expression: first, that there should be pain-behaviour without pain (304), second, that there should be pain without pain-behaviour (281). Whereas, if the recognition of pain intervened between pain and its expression, there would seem to be two further possible sources of discrepancy: inaccurate expression of correct recognition, and accurate expression of incorrect recognition. Wittgenstein argues that these are not in fact genuine possibilities. ' "Imagine a person whose memory could not retain *what* the word 'pain' meant—so that he constantly called different things by that name—but nevertheless used the word in a way fitting in with the usual symptoms and presuppositions of pain"—in short he uses it as we all do. Here I should like to say: a wheel that can be turned though nothing else moves with it, is not part of the mechanism' (271).

In general, Wittgenstein advises us, 'always get rid of the idea of the private object in this way: assume that it constantly changes, but that you do not notice the change because your memory constantly deceives you' (*PI*, II, p. 207). If inaccurate recognition and inaccurate expression were combined, there might in fact be *no* discrepancy between sensation and its expression. In that case, a man in pain who says, 'I am in pain', may be making two mistakes which cancel each other out. He may be mistaking his pain for a pleasure, and mistakenly thinking that the word 'pain' means pleasure. In fact, Wittgenstein argues, for it to be possible for an utterance to be mistaken, it must be possible to distinguish the criterion for the content of an utterance from the criterion for its truth. But in the case of an utterance in a private language no such distinction is possible. One is forced to say, 'Whatever is going to seem right to me is right'.

And 'that only means that here we can't talk about "right"' (258). In reality, according to Wittgenstein, 'what I do is not . . . to identify my sensation by criteria: but to repeat an expression. But this is not the *end* of the language-game: it is the beginning' (290; cf. 377 ff.).

The parallel with the argument I used against Descartes will now be obvious. The confused judgement about pain which is made by the man unpurified by Cartesian doubt corresponds to the use of 'I am in pain' in a public language in connection with bodily causes and manifestations of pain. The Cartesian *cogitatio*, stripped of the obscure judgement, corresponds to the private sensation disconnected from bodily expression. The perception of the *cogitatio* corresponds to the identification of the sensation by criteria. The judgement of the purified Cartesian about his clear and distinct perception corresponds to the utterance of the name for the sensation in the private language.

I said earlier that if a Cartesian spirit uses a language at all, it seems that it must be a private language. But, for Descartes, need judgements be made in language at all? Commonly, we gather, they are. 'Because we attach all our conceptions to words for the expression of them by speech, and as we commit to memory our thoughts in connection with these words; and as we more easily recall to memory words than things, we can scarcely conceive of anything so distinctly as to be able to separate completely that which we conceive from the words chosen to express the same' (*AT* VIII, 37). None the less, the philosopher can, and should, separate the conceptions from the words in which it is clothed. It might thus be thought that Descartes could escape the argument derived from Wittgenstein's critique of private language. This, however, would be a mistake. Whether a judgement is made in language or not, there must be some feature of it which makes it the particular judgement that it is. There must be something to distinguish the judgement that p from the judgement that q. And this is enough to let the argument proceed. Wherever Wittgenstein's argument talks of 'knowing the meaning of an expression' we can substitute 'recognizing the judgement for the judgement that it is'. Just as Wittgenstein's argument turned on there being no way of recognizing the meaning of an utterance in a private language independently of its truth, so the anti-Cartesian argument depended in part on there being no way of recognizing the content of a judgement independently of knowing its truth. In each case, the possibility of error gets ruled out and so the supposition of correctness becomes vacuous.

It is sometimes said that all Wittgenstein's argument shows is that it would be impossible to *learn* the words for sensations if sensations had no bodily expression. If that were so, Descartes would seem to be able to avoid criticism by pleading that the knowledge exercised in the perception of sensations was innate. But in fact Wittgenstein's argument seeks to show that it is impossible to give a coherent account of the *exercise* of the knowledge of the meaning of a word in a private language. He does not explicitly consider innate ideas; but in 257 he makes clear that his argument does not depend on considerations about learning when he says: ' "What would it be like if human beings showed no outward signs of pain (did not groan, grimace, etc.)? Then it would be impossible to teach a child the use of the word 'tooth-ache' ."—Well, let's assume the child is a genius and itself invents a name for the sensation!'

If I am right, neither the postulation of non-linguistic judgements about sensations nor the doctrine of innate ideas can save Descartes from the criticisms suggested by the passages that I have quoted from Wittgenstein. If this is so, then the argument against private languages has an importance which transcends any parochial concerns of ordinary language philosophy and the disputable theories of meaning put forward in the *Philosophical Investigations*.

APPENDIX

THE HISTORY OF INTENTION IN ETHICS

1. *The concept of intention.* Intentions are relevant to the moral and legal assessment of a man's life and deeds in three main ways. First, we need to know which of his actions and omissions were intentional and which were not; second, we may inquire with what intention he did what he did; third, we may be interested not only in the actions he performed, but also in those he intended to perform, whether or not his intentions were ever carried out.

Suppose that the movement of A's body has caused the death of B. What further is needed for it to be the case that A intentionally killed B? First, we must ask whether A's body originated its own movement, or whether it was merely passive like the body of a passenger in a crashing aircraft. If A's body was self-moving, we must further ask whether A was in possession of his faculties at the time, or whether he was temporarily or permanently deprived of their use, whether through some previous action of his (as in sleep or intoxication) or through no fault of his own (as in insanity). If he was awake, sober, and in his right mind, we must ask whether he knew or suspected that what he was doing would lead to the other's death. If not, then he killed either by mistake or by accident: such killing, if negligent, may be blameworthy, but it is not intentional.

At this point differences of opinion appear among philosophers and lawyers concerning the concept of intention. All agree that for an action to be intentional the agent must in some sense have the knowledge or suspicion that he is performing it. Some consider that for an action to be intentional the agent must also want to perform it: not necessarily desire it for its own sake, or take pleasure in it, but choose it at least as a means to some furher end. Others consider it sufficient that the agent should have some degree of knowledge, without requiring any volitional element. Some of this school require that the knowledge should amount to certainty, others are satisfied with probability, and others again are willing to impute to an agent knowledge, and with it intention, in circumstances when he lacks it but a reasonable man would have possessed it. These disagreements will be discussed below.

The intention *with which* an act is performed is a topic closely connected with that of practical reasoning. If someone is asked why he is doing a certain action, he may reply by characterizing the action itself, as in some way desirable (e.g. as pleasant, interesting, or noble) or by showing it to be a means to a desirable end. Either type of answer gives a reason for his action; the latter type of answer indicates the intention with which he performs it. In English we speak of 'doing A *in order to* do B' or 'doing A *for the sake of* doing B'. In most systems of morality the moral quality of the intention with which an act is done may make a difference to the moral quality of the act itself. Many legal systems include specific further intentions in the definitions of certain crimes, as burglary used to be defined as breaking and entering a dwelling house at night with the intent to commit a felony therein. Moralists have discussed such questions as 'Does a bad intention turn an otherwise good act into a bad one?' and 'Does the end justify the means?'

Closely connected with this sense of *intention* is the concept of *motive*. Often the words 'motive' and 'intention' do not differ in meaning but merely call up different pictures. The agent's reasons for acting may be viewed as something behind him pushing him on or something in front of him presenting him a target: thus Austin wrote "The intention is the aim of the act of which the motive is the spring'. Commonly, to explain a man's action by the future state of affairs he wishes to procure is to give his intention; to assign a reason describing the state of affairs obtaining before his action is to give his motive. Frequently an explanation by motive (e.g. 'out of friendship', 'out of greed') may subsume a particular intention ('to help Jones', 'to make another $1,000,000') under a general heading of frequent application; and as the examples show, in so doing it may or may not imply a value judgement about the intention in question. Lawyers sometimes use 'motive' to mean 'intention to perform an action with which the law does not concern itself'. Thus, if a man breaks into a house to steal money to buy medicine for his wife, he has an intent to steal, but to buy medicine is his motive. For larceny is forbidden by law, but not the purchase of medicine. In this sense it is true by definition that motives are irrelevant in law.

The topic of *intention for the future* has seemed problematic to philosophers, since the connection between such intention and its execution appears both to be contingent (not all intentions are executed) and to be necessary (to have, express, or recognize an intention to X it seems one must possess the concept of X-ing). The solution to this problem seems to be that the relationship between the intention to X, and X-ing, in general is noncontingent; and the relationship between the intention to X on a particular occasion and X-ing on that occasion is of the following kind: if a man intends to X on occasion C, and does not X on C when he can do so, some explanation is called for. Legal systems have rarely taken account of bare intentions that find no expression in action; moral systems frequently do so.

2. *Old Testament.* The distinction between intentional and non-intentional actions in different moral and legal systems can be studied in relation to homicide. The Old Testament is a case in point. The Code of the Covenant distinguished between a man 'who has dared to kill his fellow by treacherous intent' and one 'who has not lain in wait, but has had his enemy delivered into his hands by God'; the latter, but not the former, is to be given sanctuary from an avenger (Exodus, 21:12-14). Similarly, a thief breaking in can be struck a mortal blow with impunity. These distinctions seem to correspond not to that between intentional and unintentional homicide, but between premeditated and unpremeditated, provoked and unprovoked killings. The death penalty is prescribed for some cases where death was caused by negligence: if an ox gores a man or woman after its owner has ignored warnings about it, ox and owner are to be put to death (Exodus, 21:29).

The Deuteronomic Code distinguishes between premeditated killing in a feud, and accidental causing of death. A man is to be allowed sanctuary, for instance, if while he is woodcutting the head slips off the handle of his axe and strikes a companion dead (Deuteronomy, 19:15). But what is to be done, one wonders, about the accidental killing of an enemy or the deliberate killing of a comrade? The Sacerdotal Code (Numbers, 35:9 ff.) is more detailed but not more explicit on this point. Perhaps the effect of the provisions was simply that no plea of accident was entertained when the victim was an enemy.

In general it is clear that God can be offended unintentionally. The Book of Numbers distinguishes between sins of inadvertence (which are forgivable through expiatory rites) and 'sins with a high hand' which are not (15:22 ff.). Particularly instructive is the ancient story of Abimelech, who had taken to bed Sara, the wife of Abraham, under the impression that she was Abraham's sister. Threatened with punishment by God in a dream, Abimelech protests that he has not touched Sara and that in any case Abraham himself said she was his sister. 'Yes, I know', God replied, 'that you did this with a clear conscience, and it was I who prevented you from sinning against me. That was why I did not let you touch her.' (Genesis, 20:6). The story is puzzling: God seems both to accept involuntary ignorance as an excuse (else why not let Abimelech touch Sara?) and yet not to accept it (else why would he be guilty if he had done so?).

The intention with which a violation of the Law takes place cannot rectify it, however upright it may be. Famous in this connection is the story of Uzzah, who stretched out his hand to the ark of God and steadied it when the oxen carrying it made it tilt. 'The anger of Yahweh blazed out against Uzzah and for this crime God struck him down on the spot and he died.' (2 Samuel, 6:6).

The decalogue forbids not only overt acts such as theft and adultery, but concludes 'You shall not covet your neighbour's house. You shall not covet your neighbour's wife.' (Exodus, 20:17).

3. *Aristotle.* The Athenian code of Draco, like the Deuteronomic code, distinguished between premeditated murder and involuntary homicide. Plato adopted the distinction in his Laws, giving as examples of involuntary homicide the death of athletes from accidental blows and the death of patients at the hands of their doctors. But he points out that some kinds of homicide fall between these categories, for instance slaying in a quarrel on the impulse of passion (Laws, IX, 863 ff.).

In the Third Book of the *Nicomachean Ethics* Aristotle draws a more detailed distinction between voluntary and involuntary actions and happenings (*hekousia* and *akousia*). It is only for what is voluntary that men are praised or blamed. Things may happen involuntarily, either through force, like being kidnapped, or through ignorance, a category which includes mistake and accident. The ignorance which makes an act involuntary and therefore inculpable is not ignorance of what one ought to do—this is itself something blameworthy—but ignorance of what one is in fact doing. Thus a man that gives away a secret he did not know was meant to be secret, or that lets off a catapult while demonstrating its use, or that kills a son in mistake for an enemy, acts involuntarily. Something is voluntary, on the other hand, if it 'has its origin in an agent who knows the particular circumstances of his action'.

'Voluntary', so understood, is close to 'intentional' as defined by those who regard knowledge without volition as sufficient for intention. Three qualifications are needed. (1) The words traditionally translated 'voluntarily' and 'involuntarily' meant in ordinary Greek 'willingly' and 'unwillingly'. This set Aristotle a problem. Suppose a man kills an enemy by mistake, and is then glad to have done so. We cannot say he killed him willingly, since he killed him unknowingly; but if we say he killed him unwillingly, this suggests he killed him reluctantly. So Aristotle sets up a third category, the non-voluntary, between the voluntary and the involuntary (1110b, 18–23). (2) Necessity and duress also present intermediate cases. If a man jettisons his cargo in a storm, or commits a crime to save his family from a tyrant's threats, then, said Aristotle, his actions are a mixed case, but closer to the voluntary case (1110a, 4). Such actions, though reluctant, seem clearly intentional, but modern lawyers have hesitated over them no less than Aristotle, and the English word 'voluntary' is, after all, as ambiguous as its Greek equivalent. In one sense, the voluntary seems a wider category than the intentional, including acts which are controllable with an effort but are not done on purpose, such as sneezing, yawning, laughing or brooding. In another sense not all intentional actions are voluntary: the cashier hands over the cash to the bank-raider intentionally but not voluntarily. (3) At the beginning of Book Three we are told that praise and blame are given only for voluntary actions; but both in law and morals a man is often held responsible for reckless and negligent actions as well as for intentional ones. Several of Aristotle's 'actions involuntary through ignorance' are cases where blame and punishment might be in order—e.g. poisoning a patient by giving him the wrong drug. In a later chapter, however, Aristotle acknowledges that ignorance due to carelessness is punishable: for instance, when people are ignorant of things in the law which they should know and are not difficult to discover (1113b, 30 ff.).

Of all Aristotle's concepts, the one which is nearest the modern everyday sense of 'intention' is that of *choice* (prohairesis), which is defined as 'a deliberative volition of things in our power'. For me to choose something, I must want it, not as an end in itself, but as the upshot of judgement based on deliberation (1113a, 11). The deliberation may be set out in the form of a practical syllogism: e.g. 'pleasure is to be pursued, this is pleasant, pursue this' (1146b, 23). Choice, though it includes a volitional as well as a cognitive element, differs from intention in several ways. First, actions performed on a sudden without deliberation are not chosen; intentional actions can be performed without deliberation, though perhaps not without a reason. Second, choice is concerned only with means and not with ends. This fits 'intention' but not 'intentional': acts done for their own sake are not done with any intention; but they are intentional *par excellence*. Third, children and animals, Aristotle says, don't make choices; but they certainly act in order to bring about certain effects. Altogether, 'choice' seems to be a grander thing than intention: its typical example is the deliberate choice of an action in pursuit of a long-term way of life.

Choice is a necessary condition for virtuous action; moreover, an action is virtuous only if chosen for virtue's sake (1105a, 31). A non-virtuous motive, then, can spoil a virtuous action; can a good intention redeem an evil one? In one place Aristotle says that men are praised when they go through something shameful or painful for great and noble objects (1110a, 21). He has often been taken to be endorsing the principle that the end justifies the means; in fact he has in mind the case where a man *puts up with* something shameful (e.g. degradation or imprisonment), not where he *does* one of the shameful things (such as adultery or murder) which he elsewhere says can never be justified (1107a, 17).

Aristotle mentions bare intention when discussing weakness of will. He asks whether it is worse to be intemperate (to do wrong on principle) or to be incontinent (to choose rightly but act wrongly through weakness). The former state is worse, he replies, involving a corruption of the principles of action. Better to have a right mind with a wrong deed than a wrong deed with a wrong mind into the bargain (1150b, 28 ff.).

4. *Christianity.* Against the Pharisees Jesus insisted that a vainglorious motive rendered religious practices worthless: his disciples are to pray, fast, and give alms in secret, not so as to attract notice from men, but so as to win a reward from the Father in heaven (Matthew, 6:1 ff.). It is sometimes said that the New Testament is concerned more with inward thoughts and less with external acts than the Old Testament. But in the Sermon on the Mount the only inner acts discussed are adulterous desires (Matthew, 5:28), already condemned in the decalogue (Exodus, 20:17). The contrast between Jesus and contemporary Pharisaism seems to be rather that Jesus regarded the Law's prohibition of sins with social consequences—a prohibition which he interpreted very rigorously (Matthew, 5:20–48)— as more important than its prescription of ritual practices (e.g. observation of the sabbath and ceremonial washing) (Matthew, 12:9 ff.; 15:10 ff.).

St. Paul regarded the perverse practices of pagans as the divinely permitted consequence of the polytheism for which they had wilfully abandoned the knowledge of the true God (Romans, 1:18 ff.). In discussing scrupulous Christians, however, he makes clear that an erroneous conscience does have certain rights. Some keep holy days, and some abstain from meat: each must be left free to hold his own opinion. 'The one who eats meat does so in honour of the Lord, since he gives thanks to God; but then the man who abstains does that too in honour of the Lord, and so he also gives God thanks....' (Romans, 14:5 ff.). Out of its context this might suggest that a good intention can justify a bad action; but in fact Paul rejects the principle 'do evil as a means to good' (Romans, 3:8). The goodness or badness of what is done in this case depends on the intention simply because the act in question is an indifferent one. 'No food is unclean in itself; however, if someone thinks that a particular food is unclean, then it is unclean for him.' (Romans, 14:14).

St. Augustine, building on St. Paul and Platonic sources,

developed a moral system which attached great importance to intention. No action, he taught, is really good unless done out of love of God and one's neighbour. 'Whatever is done either for fear of punishment, or with some other unspiritual motive . . . is not done as it ought to be, however much it may seem well done.' (*Enchiridion*, ch. 32). For a good action, then, love is a necessary motive: is it also sufficient? No: when Augustine said 'Love, and do as you please' he did not mean that there was no action which love could not justify, but that one who loved God and his neighbour would never want to perform acts prohibited by the moral law. In this he was echoing Paul: 'All the commandments, You shall not commit adultery, you shall not kill, you shall not steal, you shall not covet, and so on, are summed up in this single command: You must love your neighbour as yourself.' (Romans, 13:9). Augustine insisted that there are some actions—lying is one—which no motive can justify (*De Doctrina Christiana*, 21). Such actions are universally unjust, independent of custom (*Retractations*, I, 13, 8). Though we must refrain from them out of love of God, it is not because God forbids them that they are wrong; rather, they are forbidden by God because they are already wrong by nature (*Contra Faustum*, 22).

5. *Abelard.* Peter Abelard's *Ethica* is notorious for the extreme importance it attaches to intention in morals. Abelard argues that sin is not in willing (*voluntas*) but in consenting (*consensus*): there can be sin without will (as when a fugitive kills in self-defence) and bad will without sin (such as lustful desires one cannot help). From his examples it is clear that by '*voluntas*' he means the desire of something for its own sake; he agrees that all sins are voluntary in the sense that they are not unavoidable and that they are the result of some volition or other—e.g. the fugitive's will to escape. '*Consensus*' and '*intentio*' are used as synonyms; the state of mind they denote involves knowledge but not desire. Abelard argues that since one can perform a prohibited act innocently—e.g. marry one's sister unaware that she is one's sister—the evil must be not in the act but in the consent. 'It is not what is done, but with what mind it is done, that God weighs; the desert and praise of the agent rests not in his action but in his intention.' (*Ethica*, 3).

Thus, a bad intention may ruin a good act. Two men may hang a criminal, one out of zeal for justice, the other out of inveterate hatred; the act is just, but one does well, the other ill. More shockingly, a good intention may justify a prohibited action. Those who were cured by Jesus did well to disobey his order to keep the cure secret, for their motive in publicizing it was a good one. God himself, when he ordered Abraham to kill his son Isaac, performed a wrong act with a right intention.

On the topic of bare intention, Abelard taught that a good intention not carried out might be as praiseworthy as a good action. If two men resolve to build an almshouse, and the first succeeds while the second is robbed of his money in advance, each is as deserving as the other. Otherwise we must say that one man may be more virtuous than another simply because he is richer (*Ethica*, 7).

Similarly, bad intentions are as blameworthy as bad actions. Why then punish actions rather than intentions? Human punishment, Abelard replies, may be justified where there is no guilt: a woman who has overlain her infant is punished to make others more careful. In general, we punish actions rather than intentions because human frailty regards a more manifest evil as a greater evil. But God will not judge thus.

Does it follow that those who persecute Christians in the belief that they serve God thereby act praiseworthily? No, says Abelard: they are no more guilty than a man who kills his fellow by mistake for an animal while hunting in a forest, but their action is not positively praiseworthy. For a man to have a good intention, it is not sufficient that a man should think he is doing well. 'The intention of the persecutors is erroneous, and their eye is not simple.' (c. 12).

Abelard seems to be confusing the persecutors' opinion about the morality of killing Christians with the virtuous purpose for which they killed them, viz. to serve God. Consequently it is not clear whether the doctrine of justification by intention means that an erroneous conscience excuses from guilt, or that a good intention justifies means known to be evil. It was Alexander of Hales who first cleared up Abelard's confusion, distinguishing the volitional element of intention from the cognitive element of conscience.

Peter Lombard, in his *Sentences*, agreed with the general rule that the goodness or badness of a man's acts depended on the goodness or badness of his intention, but made an exception to this general rule of those actions declared by Augustine to be evil in themselves. Some of Abelard's followers denied that such cases provided real counter-examples. To steal in order to give to the poor, for instance, was not a case of a bad act with a good motive; the intention, fully described, was 'to give other people's money to the poor' and that was an evil intention (IV *Sent.*, 2, 40).

St. Bonaventure, commenting on the *Sentences*, introduced a new point. For an act to be good it was not sufficient that it should be an act of an unprohibited kind done with a good intention; it was necessary that the end be a greater good than the means. To preach the gospel was a good thing; to earn one's bread was a good thing; but to preach the gospel in order to earn one's bread was not a good thing (*In II Sent.*, 38.1.1).

6. *Aquinas.* Aquinas' treatment of voluntariness in the *Summa Theologiae* (Ia IIae, 6) followed in its main lines the recently discovered *Nicomachean Ethics*. 'The voluntary includes not only what we want as an end in itself, but also what we want for the sake of some other end' (loc. cit., art 6 ad 1); but something can be voluntary without being the result of any positive act, as when the sinking of a ship is attributed to its captain's negligence (loc. cit., art 3). The voluntary is therefore a broader category than the intentional. Intention is defined as an act of the will concerning a goal for the sake of which something is done. 'In order to be said to intend health, it is not sufficient to want it; you must want to achieve it by means of something else' (Ia IIae, 12, 1 ad 4). A typical expression of intention is 'I want medicine for the sake of health'; in such a case the end is the reason for wanting the means (loc. cit., art 4). The end is *wanted*, the means are *chosen*; what is *intended* is neither the end in itself nor the means in themselves, but the end *through* the means (Ia IIae, 13).

Human acts may be divided into kinds, some of which are good (e.g. using one's own property) some bad (e.g. stealing), some indifferent (e.g. walking in the country). Every concrete action, however, will be performed in particular circumstances with a particular purpose. For an action to be good, the kind it belongs to must not be bad, the circumstances must be appropriate, and the intention must be virtuous. If any of these elements is missing the act is evil. Consequently, a bad intention can spoil a good act (almsgiving out of vainglory) but a good intention cannot redeem a bad act (stealing to give to the poor) (Ia IIae, 18, 4; 18, 9; 20, 2).

Aquinas considers separately the problem of erroneous conscience. To do what one thinks wrong is always wrong; it is always bad for a man's will to disaccord with his reason, even if his reason is in error (Ia IIae, 19, 5). But though an erroneous conscience always binds, it does not always excuse. If a mistake, whether of morality or of fact, is due to negligence, then the agent is not excused. Adultery is not excused by thinking it lawful, for such error is culpable ignorance of the law of God. But a man who without negligence believes another man's wife to be his own does not sin by intercourse with her (Ia IIae, 19, 6).

Aquinas agrees with Abelard that the goodness of a good action derives from the good will with which it is performed; but he says that will can only be good if willing an action of a kind reason can approve (Ia IIae, 20, 1). Moreover he insists that good will cannot be fully genuine (*perfecta*) unless it is put into action when opportunity arises. A failure to act must be an involuntary failure if it is to be irrelevant to morality (Ia IIae, 20, 4). Thus Abelard's paradoxical conclusions are avoided.

The morality of an act, Aquinas says, may be affected by its consequences. A bad consequence of a bad act, if foreseen, makes the act worse; if not foreseen, it will make it worse only if it is a natural and regular consequence (*per se et ut in pluribus*). (Ia IIae, 20a5c). In discussing the consequences of sin, Aquinas distinguishes between the harm which is foreseen and intended, and that which is foreseen and not intended. As an example of the former he cites the harm resulting from the actions of a murderer or thief; to illustrate the latter he says 'A man, crossing a field the more easily to fornicate, may damage what is sown in the field, knowingly, but without a mind to do any damage'. In both cases, he says, the sin is aggravated by the amount of harm done, but in the second only indirectly. A man may be punished as negligent for harm neither foreseen nor intended, if the action causing it was itself unlawful (Ia IIae, 73, 8).

The difference between direct and indirect aggravation of sin is unclear: does direct aggravation justify greater punishment? Moreover, we are left uncertain about the responsibility of an agent for the harmful consequences of his good or indifferent actions.

The unclarity persists when Aquinas applies his doctrine to homicide, and in particular to killing in self-defence (IIa IIae, 64, 7). Augustine had taught that this was forbidden for a Christian; the Decretals said it was lawful to repel force with force. Aquinas says: an act may have two effects, one intended, the other beside the intention; the act of a man defending himself may have two effects, one the preservation of his own life, the other the death of the attacker. Provided no more violence is used than necessary, such an act is permissible; however, it is never lawful to *intend* to kill another, unless one is acting on public authority like a soldier or policeman. In the context it is not clear whether Aquinas is justifying accidental killing in the course of a struggle or intentional killing when this is the only way to avoid being killed.

7. *Double effect and direction of intention.* The gaps in Aquinas' account were filled in by the 16th-century theologians of Salamance who developed the famous doctrine of double effect. The doctrine is stated thus by John of St. Thomas (*De Bonitate et Malitia Actuum Humanorum*). If an act, not evil in itself, has both good and bad effects, then it may be permissible if (1) the evil effect is not intended; (2) the good effect is not produced by means of the bad; (3) on balance, the good done outweighs the harm. So stated, the doctrine is sensible enough and has many everyday applications: e.g. it is all right to appoint the best man to a job, though you know that by doing so you will give pain to the other candidates.

What gave the doctrine of double effect a bad name was its association with the theory of direction of intention satirized by Pascal in the *Lettres Provinciales*. Whatever Aquinas meant by saying that you could not intend to kill in self-defence, he was taken by theologians to mean that you could kill in self-defence provided you fixed your attention on the defensive, rather than the lethal, aspect of what you were doing (Layman, 1624). Not intending to kill in this special theological sense is, of course, perfectly compatible with intending to kill in the ordinary sense (Windass, 1963). Pascal makes his imaginary Jesuit say 'Our method of direction of intention consists in proposing to oneself, as the end of one's actions, a permitted object. As far as we can we turn men away from forbidden things, but when we cannot prevent the action at least we purify the intention'. Thus, for instance, you may kill in return for an insult. 'All you have to do is to turn your intention from the desire for vengeance, which is criminal, to the desire to defend one's honour, which is permitted.' (*Seventh Letter*). Such direction of intention is simply a performance in imagination which has little to do with the means one chooses to one's ends; if conjoined with the principle of double effect it makes that principle indistinguishable in practice from justification of the means by the end.

8. *Kant*. Neither the continental rationalists nor the British empiricists devoted great attention to the topics so far discussed. But in the moral philosophy of Kant motive occupies a place parallel to that which it occupied in the moral theology of Augustine. Nothing, he says in the *Groundwork of the Metaphysics of Morals*, is unqualifiedly good except a good will, which is good not because of what it effects or accomplishes, but simply in itself, even if 'through the niggardly endowment of stepmotherly nature' it is entirely lacking in power to carry out its intentions. A man's will has this goodness only if his motive is the motive of duty. A shopkeeper may be honest because honesty pays; a benevolent person may help others because he enjoys doing so. The actions of these people may be in accordance with their duty; but unless they act not from inclination, but from duty, they fall short of the highest moral worth. The test of the moral value of an action is not the purpose of the action, in the sense of the state of affairs to be realized by it. Rather, it is the maxim in accordance with which it is decided upon. I ought never to act except in such a way that I can also will that my maxim should become a universal law. This is the test by which I can tell whether I act out of duty, i.e. out of pure reverence for the moral law. Kant admits that perhaps no action has ever had so pure and lofty a motive; possibly for this reason, he does not care to develop a casuistry of intention to discriminate between various ways in which actions may fall short of the ideal.

9. *The Utilitarians*. Kant exalted motive more than any other moral philosopher; the Utilitarians, said J. S. Mill, 'have gone beyond almost all others in affirming that the motive has nothing to do with the morality of the action'. Their founder, Jeremy Bentham, however, in his *Principles of Morals and Legislation*, expounded the concept of intention more lucidly than any previous writer. He used the word 'intentional' in the sense

commonly expressed by 'voluntary'; the latter word, he said, was misleading since it sometimes meant *uncoerced* and sometimes *spontaneous*. An act, he said, might be intentional without its consequences being so: 'thus, you may intend to touch a man without intending to hurt him: and yet, as the consequences turn out, you may chance to hurt him.' A consequence may be either directly intentional ('when the prospect of producing it constituted one of the links in the chain of causes by which the person was determined to act') or obliquely intentional (when the consequence was foreseen as likely, but the prospect of producing it formed no link in the determining chain). An incident which is directly intentional may be either ultimately or mediately intentional, depending whether the prospect of producing it would or would not have operated as a motive if not viewed as productive of a further event. The distinction between direct and oblique intention corresponds to the scholastic one between intention and foresight; the distinction between ultimate and mediate intention to that between end and means.

According to Bentham it is misleading to speak of good and bad intentions. 'If (an intention) be deemed good or bad in any sense, it must be either because it is deemed to be productive of good or of bad consequences or because it is deemed to originate from a good or from a bad motive.' Now consequences depend on circumstances; circumstances are no part of the object of a man's intention; they are simply either known to him or unknown to him. So whatever is to be said of the goodness or badness of a man's intention as resulting from the consequences of his act depends on his knowledge ('consciousness') of the circumstances (Ch. VIII).

If a man is aware of a circumstance when he acts, then his act is said to have been an *advised* act, with respect to that circumstance; otherwise an *unadvised* act. Besides being unaware of circumstances which actually obtain, an agent may suppose circumstances to obtain which actually do not; this is *missupposal* and makes an act *misadvised*. A circumstance missupposed may be *preventive* (i.e. if it had obtained the evil would have been prevented) or *compensative* (if it had obtained the evil would have been outweighed by good consequences).

If an act is intentional, and is advised with respect to all circumstances relevant to a particular consequence, and there is

APPENDIX

no missupposal of preventive circumstances, then the consequence is intentional. 'Advisedness, with respect to the circumstances, if clear from the missupposal of any preventive circumstance, extends the intentionality from the act to the consequences.' (Ch IX).

An act which is unadvised may be *heedless*, and one which is misadvised may be *rash*. An act is termed heedless or rash when the case is thought to be such that a person of ordinary prudence and ordinary benevolence would have been likely to have sufficiently attended to, or reflected on, the circumstances as to have been disposed to prevent the mischief in question.

Bentham distinguishes between intentions and motives: a man's intentions may be good and his motives bad. For a man's intention to be good it is sufficient that the consequences of his action would have been good if they had turned out as he foresaw. For instance 'out of malice a man prosecutes you for a crime of which he believes you to be guilty, but of which in fact you are not guilty'. The intention here is good, because though the actual consequences are mischievous and the motive is evil, the consequences envisaged were good (Ch. IX.)

In discussing motives Bentham stresses the evaluative overtones of words such as 'lust', 'avarice', and 'cruelty'. In itself, he says, no motive is either good or bad; these words denote bad motives only in the sense that they are never properly applied except where the motives they signify happen to be bad. 'Lust', for instance, was the name given to sexual desire when the effects of it were regarded as bad. Though motives, neutrally described, can be roughly classified as good, bad, or indifferent, according to the common complexion of their effects, it is strictly only in individual cases that motives can be good or bad. 'A motive is good, when the intention it gives birth to is a good one; bad, when the intention is a bad one; and an emotion is good or bad according to the material consequences that are the objects of it.' (Ch. X).

By 'motive' Bentham means what he would otherwise call an ultimately and directly intentional consequence, described in neutral terms. From his explanation it is clear that it does not supply a separate title of moral qualification of an act; the only mental state primarily relevant to the morality of a voluntary act is the cognitive state with regard to the consequences. This is in accord with the general Utilitarian position concerning moral goodness and badness in actions, which is judged in terms of their consequences in terms of pleasure and pain. An act, however, which has mischievous consequences, may also effect a secondary mischief, such as alarm or danger. And this, Bentham says, may be affected by the motive: some states of mind are more dangerous and alarming than others.

J. S. Mill summed up lucidly the Utilitarian position on motives. 'He who saves a fellow-creature from drowning does what is morally right, whether his motive be duty, or the hope of being paid for his trouble; he who betrays the friend that trusts him is guilty of a crime, even if his object be to serve another friend to whom he is under greater obligation.' One motive may be preferable to another on non-moral grounds; or because it may proceed from a quality of character more likely to produce virtuous acts in the long term. But in general 'the motive has nothing to do with the morality of the action, though much with the worth of the agent'. (*Utilitarianism*, Ch. 2).

10. *Intention and the Law*. The maxim of common law *actus non facit reum nisi mens sit rea* insists that no act can be criminal unless accompanied by a certain mental state. But the state of mind which constitutes *mens rea* varies from crime to crime. Let us suppose that the law wishes to prohibit a certain action, which it describes without reference to the agent's state of mind (e.g. using a motor vehicle uninsured). The law may wish this *actus reus* to be punishable (1) no matter whether the agent did know or could have known he was doing it; (2) no matter whether he did know, but only if he could have known he was doing it; (3) no matter whether he wanted to do it, but only if he knew or thought likely that he was doing it; (4) only if he wanted to do it, either for its own sake, or for some unspecified further purpose; (5) only if he wanted to do it for some further purpose specified in the law.

In the first case, there is no *mens rea* at all, and the law will be one of strict liability: such is the English statute forbidding the sale of adulterated milk. In the second case, the crime will be one of negligence: negligence resulting in death constitutes one species of the common law crime of manslaughter.

Cases (3), (4), and (5) are the ones relevant to intention. The third case would be called by Bentham obliquely intentional; some contemporary lawyers prefer to call it reckless unless the

APPENDIX 145

knowledge involved amounts to certainty (Williams, 1966). All agree, however, that this degree of *mens rea* is sufficient to constitute murder in English or American law. In the case of *R.* v. *Desmond* (1868) a Fenian conspirator was found guilty of murder because, by dynamiting the wall of Clerkenwell prison to liberate two imprisoned fellow-conspirators, he had caused the deaths of persons living near-by. In summing up, Lord Coleridge said 'It is murder if a man did an act not with the purpose of taking life but with the knowledge or belief that life was likely to be sacrificed' (Hart, 1967). Indeed, it suffices that there be knowledge of the likelihood of grievous bodily harm (e.g. *R.* v. *Vickers* (1957).)

How far can this knowledge be presumed? It has long been a maxim that 'a man must be taken to intend the natural consequences of his acts' (e.g. Day, J. in *Gayford* v. *Chouler* (1898), 1. Q.B. 316—a case in which the appellant had damaged the respondent's grass by walking across his field). But the presumption was made an irrebuttable one in English murder law by the decision in *D. P. P.* v. *Smith* (1961), A. C. 290. Smith was driving a car containing stolen property when ordered by a policeman to draw into a curb. He accelerated and zigzagged the car as the constable clung to its side; the car collided with four oncoming vehicles, the fourth of which ran over and killed the policeman. Smith was convicted of murder; the conviction was quashed on appeal but restored by the House of Lords. The effect of the Lords' judgement was that if a reasonable man would have foreseen grievous bodily harm as the consequence of an unlawful act, then the agent is guilty of murder when death results, no matter what he himself foresaw or did not foresee.

The judgement was much criticized, and a reform of the law was suggested in a report of the Law Commission (1967). This suggested that no court or jury should be bound to infer that a man intended or foresaw the natural and probable consequence of his actions. It also recommended that killing shall not amount to murder unless done with intent to kill; a man has such an intent 'if he means his actions to kill, or if he is willing for his actions, though meant for another purpose, to kill in accomplishing that purpose'.

The first but not the second of these recommendations was embodied in the Criminal Justice Act of 1967. If the second recommendation had been accepted death which was obliquely intentional would still count as murder: for if one fails to desist from a course of action one knows is likely to cause death, then one is willing for one's actions to kill in accomplishing one's purposes. The Law Commission's proposal, therefore, fell short of their avowed aim of bringing legal terminology into accord with ordinary language. For ordinarily a man would be said to intend his actions only in the fourth case listed above, when the result is not only foreseen but wanted as a means or end. Thus, a man who rises in the night for a drink may know that he will wake the baby without intending to wake the baby.

The law does distinguish between direct and oblique intention in cases which come under the fifth head above. Nothing in law corresponds to the way in which a good act may be morally vitiated by a bad intention. As Macaulay said, if a man does a socially desirable act, it is absurd for a tribunal to inquire into his motives with a view to punishing him if he did it out of malice (Williams, 1966). But a criminal intention may make an innocent act criminal (e.g. loitering with intent) or make an offence more serious (e.g. wounding with intent to kill carries a severer penalty than simple wounding). In such cases, oblique intention is insufficient: for instance, one does not commit the crime of doing an act likely to assist the enemy with the intention of assisting the enemy if the assistance to the enemy is merely foreseen and in no way desired (*R. v. Steane*, (1947), K.B. 997). Similarly, to commit the crime of attempted murder, one must act *in order to* kill, and not simply act foreseeing death as a likely outcome. It is still a matter of dispute whether there are any utilitarian grounds for applying a distinction between direct and oblique intention in law. Some would have the law of murder reformed to take account of the distinction, others would have the law of attempt reformed in order to obliterate it (Williams, 1966; Kenny, 1966; Hart, 1967).

It is generally regarded as tyrannous for the law to interest itself in unexecuted intentions that have not led to action. 'So long as an act rests in bare intention alone it is not punishable by our law' said Lord Mansfield in 1784. To attempt to enforce any such law would involve too great an infringement of liberty with little hope of success (Hart, 1967).

BIBLIOGRAPHY

In addition to the primary sources mentioned in the text the following works have been drawn on and will be found useful. On the philosophical concept of intention: G. E. M. Anscombe, *Intention*, Oxford, 1957. On intention in the Old Testament: P. T. Van Imschoot, *Theologie de l'Ancien Testament*, Paris, 1956, 227 ff. On Aristotle: G. E. M. Anscombe, 'Thought and Action in Aristotle', in R. Bambrough (ed.) *New Essays in Plato and Aristotle*, London, 1965. On the New Testament: C. A. Pierce, *Conscience in the New Testament*, London, 1955. On St. Augustine: E. Portalié, *A Guide to the Thought of St. Augustine*, Chicago, 1960, 270 ff. On Abelard and his successors: E. Lottin, *Psychologie et Morale aux XII et XIII siècles*, IV, 309-486. On Aquinas and Bentham: E. D'Arcy, *Human Acts*, Oxford, 1963. On the principle of double effect: S. Windass, 'Double Think and Double Effect'. *Blackfriars* XLIV (1963), 257 ff. On intention in the law: G. Williams, *Criminal Law, the General Part*, London, 1960, 9 ff. and *The Mental Element in Crime*, Jerusalem, 1965; Lord Denning, *Responsibility before the Law*, Jerusalem, 1961; A. Kenny, 'Intention and Purpose', *Journal of Philosophy* LXIII, (1966), 642 ff., reprinted with emendations in Summers, *Essays on Legal Philosophy*, Oxford, 1968; H. L. A. Hart, 'Intention and Punishment', *Oxford Review* 4 (1967); R. Cross, 'The Mental Element in Crime', *Law Quarterly Review* (1967), 215 ff.; The Law Commission, *Imputed Criminal Intent*, London, 1967.